TAINTED DNA

Pursuing Our True Spiritual Design

*A path to better awareness of your
intended meaningful life.*

MICHAEL V. GORDON

Snow Owl
—PUBLISHING—

ISBN 978-1-7338807-0-1

First printing 2019
Book design by Najdan Mancic, Iskon Design

Contents

Our lives were never meant to be this difficult. Unfortunately, our lives became very arduous due to a couple of ancient ancestors in the Garden of Eden who chose to disobey the Creator of all things. First the woman (Eve) was deceived, and then the man (Adam) chooses her over the Divine. This action creates a cascade of punishing, back-breaking and painful events that carries on to this very day.

As a result of one decision, mankind was separated from having an unmitigated and total relationship with God. The "freewill" provided to man proved too immense for mankind to grasp. Man was in an early stage of spiritual awareness and the fallen angel Lucifer/Satan proved too masterful at the art of manipulation and deceit. Already at war with God, Satan has been expelled from heaven for attempting to wrestle control of the universe from God, and sets his wrath for the Almighty toward destroying the "special" creation of God – mankind. Satan decides while he may lose the war, he will win small battles by destroying every human soul he can. In this way, Satan is basically shaking his fist and offending the Creator with every single sinful act that mankind performs.

The purpose of this book is to show how God can work with a man (me) as his tool to help explain what in the world happened to us, who He really is, and reminding us of His path toward eternal salvation. I've attempted to illuminate, through many scriptures, what we should know, and what we may want to consider in order to establish a better relationship with God going forward. This work expresses in "plain" easy to understand language why and how we can benefit from a personal relationship with the Heavenly Father through His Son, Jesus.

Writings, such as this one, provide us with biblical truths to help all of us begin or strengthen our walk with the Lord. I hope you will come away better informed as a result of reading this book.

Michael V. Gordon

ACKNOWLEDGMENTS

Our Heavenly Father, Our Lord Jesus and the Holy Spirit presented the vision for this book from the very beginning. The words of King Solomon provided inspiration in Ecclesiastes 1:9, "What has been will be again, what has been done will be done again; there is nothing new under the sun." Meaning everything that is being said here undoubtedly has been said before — but reminders can't hurt.

My friend Les for letting me include a portion of his life story and listening to me express my need to write this book. The editors, book designer and book formatting professionals for all their patience and tedious work to help make this book the best it can be. Any shortcomings are mine alone. Thank you all!

Most of all, my loving and supporting wife, Cindy, who understands I'm a passionate quirky guy and lets me do my thing with only an occasional rolling of the eyes. As well as my beautiful and talented daughters, Ashleigh, Alexis and Allyson who have brought me so much joy, and are always thinking of my well-being. Linda Gordon, my mother, who gave me wonderful support throughout my life. I love you all!

INTRODUCTION

Even the most astute believer struggles with the concepts and meaning of God's Word. No amount of time in the Word or diplomas from bible colleges will come close to bringing a full understanding to all of who God is. We will never fully comprehend the mind of our Creator or the intricacies of the bible for the mere fact that we are human and God is God.

WE ALL NEED TO HEAR THINGS WE DON'T WANT TO HEAR AND LEARN ABOUT THINGS WE DIDN'T KNOW.

It is in the place of exhale and peacefulness, a nearness to God and His love that allows for relaxed contemplation of what is often too complex to understand. It is the time we set aside for the Lord that allows for our heart to feel loved rather than condemned, calm rather than anxious. It is with the utmost desire that the words within this book will allow the reader to truly hear the Word of God being presented and to apply them to their lives. The words contained herein are presented to hopefully lead the reader to an understanding that a true everlasting life is possible despite the polluted DNA that currently separates us from a "complete" relationship with the Creator. The bridge to complete the relationship is found in believing and following Christ.

I, just like you, am a sinner—which is to admit that my DNA is polluted with every sort of self- serving desire toward wrongdoing, corruption, perversion, iniquity, and immorality. If it weren't for my faith in God I have no doubt I could be a rather foul and depraved person. I know that my walk with God is all that keeps me from being totally immoral, full of vice and gross misconduct.

Contained within the Bible is a small book called Titus, which is a letter written by the Apostle Paul to his friend, Titus. In Titus 3:3 it states the following:

*"At one time we too were **foolish, disobedient, deceived and enslaved** by all kinds of passions and pleasures. We lived in malice and envy, being hated and hating one another."*

That about sums up my life, and that of every person who has been gifted the grace of God. The question is, are you ready to live a more complete life? If the answer is yes, I think I may be able to assist you in some small way.

You see, over the years of my life, I came to realize that I was presented with a calling to use a "gift" that had been given to me from the Almighty. I did not ask for the gift, but it became increasingly clear when I would speak to others about

11

spiritual matters that I had more of a "sensitive" nature or ability most did not seem to possess when it came to divine affairs. I, like many others over their lifetimes, chose to ignore or not take action about really using the gift. I was too busy doing whatever pleased me to the point that God would just have to wait until I decided I was ready! Well, God basically told me He wasn't going to wait any longer—so let's just say He did some things that got my full attention. So I started writing what I believed He wanted me to say.

I have written this book to hopefully help anyone seeking to better understand God and His plans and to assist the reader in ultimately knowing more about their own existence. However, neither I nor anyone else can FULLY understand all of God's plans. I am frequently humbled by what little I really do know about His plans. Yet I soldier on and attempt to take complex themes from the Bible and to put words together to aid someone who is searching for ways to build or strengthen their relationship with the Creator. By no means do I believe I have all the answers, and I am quite willing to admit I actually have no idea of some of the things that God has done or will do. I am not a prophet—heck I'm not even a formal biblical interpreter. Quite simply I am an "explainer". Just a guy with a way to explain somewhat complex things in a more simply-worded manner which seems to accommodate the minds of some people who desire to better understand the meaning of spiritual experiences expressed in the Holy Scriptures.

As I just stated, fully knowing and understanding all of God's plans are impossible for the capacity of the human mind, including mine. Nor is the way that you or I may choose to approach the meaning of all things—including mankind's role—the way God decides to approach that same issue. God truly does work in mysterious ways!

He reminds us of this in his words to the prophet Isaiah in *Isaiah 55:8-9*

"This plan of mine is not what you would work out, neither are my thoughts the same as yours. For just as the heavens are higher than the earth, so are my ways higher than yours, and my thoughts than your thoughts."

You need to *remember* this scripture as you read the rest of this book, as well as the Bible, so that you do not attempt to put God in a human "box". It has never worked and it never will work!

I want to make it known that I don't possess any degrees in theology. I don't even profess to be more intelligent than most, including you. Again, I'm just a guy who understands some stuff in the Bible a little better than many other folks, and can for some, "explain" the scriptures in a way that is easier to comprehend. As a result, I enjoy assisting others to begin, or continue, their walk with the Lord. It is my sincerest desire that I do not mislead anyone and that if my views are later found to contain mistakes that the Lord forgives me for my mistakes. I will humbly make any corrections if I find that my interpretations are in error. I have prayed that the Lord lead me in all that I write and present.

I am, nonetheless, confident that if you will read the information presented, with prayers to God to open your mind, you will learn and more will be revealed to you of what is contained in the Scriptures. In addition, you will be putting on "the armor" of God that you may need to deflect erroneous beliefs that our adversary Satan uses in order to confound us at every opportunity. Furthermore, you may become more persuasive in your speech in accomplishing the ultimate—bringing others (new disciples) to know God the Father and our Lord and Savior Jesus Christ. In Hosea 6:6 God says "I don't want your sacrifices—I want your love. I don't want your offerings—**I want you to know me.**"

Once we truly know God, He wants us to share this knowledge with anyone who is desiring a better and more complete life.

The Bible is the best way to learn about God and what He wants from you. I heard a pastor once say that the Bible addressed three important questions that people want to know:

1. What does the Bible say?
2. What does the Bible mean?
3. What will the Bible be able to do for you?

In a nutshell, God, through his Son Jesus, wants to have a very personal relationship with you. He wants you to know who He is and why you need Him guiding your life. He wants you to know He loves you and He desires to receive your love in return. He wants you to fear Him, which really means for you to understand and respect His awesome power. He wants you to be merciful to others just as He provides mercy to you. He wants your praise through worship so that you publicly show you belong to Him. He wants your acknowledgment that Jesus is your Lord and Savior who died for your sins and conquered death by rising from the dead. He wants you to then share His story with others to help them make their lives more meaningful.

By reading this book, it is my belief that you will better know God, and you will love Him for what has been, and is being done for you! However, you must open your mind and stop allowing yourself to be deceived by the evil one, who wants nothing more than to keep us from believing and knowing the Father through his Son, Jesus. **2 Corinthians 5:7 states "We know these things are true by believing, not by seeing."** It is very difficult for many highly-educated people to understand this. They are caught in the trap that human intelligence and more education makes more sense than to follow God and put their trust in Him. They continually over-rely on their brain and under-rely on their heart/mind. It is like the person you know who must always make things more complicated than they should be. This type of person can't seem to "sense" what seems best, and instead they continually need more data, knowledge, proof or whatever to accept another position other than the one they have ingrained in their mind. Spiritually they seem to be desensitized because they do not fully understand that Satan is real and that he uses every worldly way, including prideful intelligence, to keep an unbeliever or partial believer at bay in knowing God in an intimate way.

However, most men and women are curious by nature. Man desires answers to how and why things work a certain way. It is difficult for mankind to simply accept things, even spiritually, just because someone in a pulpit, or a friend, or the Bible tells them that they should. Most people want answers that have some semblance of logic and/or have information presented that contains some basis of facts or at the very least a "feeling" that what is being shared with them is entirely plausible. A debate is healthful in matters of spirituality unless it is taken to the point of a disrespectful, obstinate argument. Before it gets to that point, a true believer should sense that the conversation is about to get out of hand and move on.

You will soon see that God's grand plan includes revealing many scientifically-accepted truths contained in His Holy Scriptures. You will begin to understand why mankind was created, why you are so special, why Satan exists, what Satan is doing, how you can continue to resist sinning, why Jesus sacrificed Himself for you, and many other things.

I am happy to see that you are taking spiritual steps, which will lead to strides along your personal path of either greater understanding, better comprehending, or eternal salvation.

It is my pursuit to simply save one soul. If I can do that, then all of this "explaining" has been worth it.

CHAPTER 1

Intentional Exploration

You are inevitably being drawn to read this because you, like most of us, are searching for answers about God, His purpose for creating you, and what His plan is for mankind. By reading this, you are taking a step, for which God is pleased to see, to better understand why you need Him as the center of your existence.

JESUS WAS SENT TO SHOW US GOD'S LOVE AND FORGIVENESS.

However, I need you to know that I wrote this as much for me as I did you. You see, God sometimes has messages even for the messenger. So while I am presenting concepts to you to hopefully help you better understand your existence and the order of things, He is also personally revealing more to me. It is truly amazing the way God works.

It is my sincerest desire that this writing serves its true purpose—to bring you into a relationship with God, to make you a disciple of Jesus, or simply to make your relationship with Him even stronger than it is currently. I believe many people want a relationship with the Creator, or a more intimate relationship with Him, but unfortunately they lack an ability to discern readily what God may be saying in his Holy Scriptures—the Bible. The Holy Scriptures can be challenging to discern even for those praying for the Holy Spirit of God to help them understand.

This is why I wrote this book. I feel as though I am compelled to, but you are welcome to believe whatever you wish about me as it does not matter. I believe that for far too long I have ignored God's desire for me to write down these words; and as a result, "things" have happened in my life to "get my attention."

As I stated previously, I was not given a choice of what "gift" I would possess because I serve His purposes—not the other way around! Gifts from God can take on many forms: prophecy, music, interpretation, healing, and many others. However, there is no choosing what your gift will be—it is what God determines.

I know that I am and will always continue to be a sinner! I will never be perfect or even close—just ask my wife. I have no desire to be placed on anyone's pedestal or to even be considered better than anyone else. I am only a human who has been given a set of "keys" to locks that open **SOME** doors and help **SOME** people better understand what God may mean. I then attempt my best to convey the meaning in simple terms that I hope resonates with most seekers. Notice again I said what He may mean—for no one can fully understand God and all His ways.

I, like every human being before me, presently existing, or who will exist in the future, am prone to making mistakes and errors. If I have any errors in this writing, I want to apologize to you for the mistake and I will readily accept the responsibility for my mistake; it is not my intent to mislead anyone. I am doing this with the sole purpose to help anyone who is seeking a greater appreciation of God. I am in the pursuit of saving one soul.

Another confession is that I, like you, and every human, do not necessarily always **CHOOSE** to exercise upon my knowledge and wisdom. I am a human being and have my own set of frailties, shortcomings, obstinance, and human desires. Thus, I have sinned so many times it is like grains of sand on a beach— immeasurable! However, I have confessed my sins to God and that is all that matters. I am forgiven for my sins through the sacred blood of Jesus Christ and my belief in Him as the Savior of the world, which I will explain in more detail later in this book. Fortunately, for all of us, the God Son Jesus washed away all of our sins with the sacrifice of His precious blood at Golgotha on the cross of crucifixion. So you are forgiven of sin, past ones, present ones and future ones through faith in believing that Jesus was not a mere mortal, but that He was born from God, delivered by a virgin woman in human form, died to wash away our sins, and conquered death through resurrection. Jesus is "alive" and sitting upon His throne awaiting the command from the Father as to the appropriate time for His return to earth—for the final judgment. I, nor you, need ever confess your sins to any man and woman, whether they be the Pope or your significant other; if you wish or want to do so, that is fine. However, it is not a requirement for salvation! Yes, God knows your sins before you confess them to Him in prayer, but He simply wants you to confess your sins as it shows that you hold Him in a position of authority and that you acknowledge accountability for your actions.

So why did God do all of this for us? That is what I intend to attempt to further explain. In short, God made man as a special creation of His design and *for His purposes*, endowed with qualities that more closely resemble God's nature than any other of his creations—including angels! In fact, we were designed by and MADE by God, while all other creatures and things were simply "thought" into existence. However, mankind, not being as intelligent as angels, was DECEIVED and has been lied to over and over by none other than Lucifer/

21

Satan/the Devil/the dragon/the evil one/Beelzebub, or any other name he is designated by in the Holy Scriptures.

Why did this all happen? Why were we created, only to be deceived by Lucifer? If you read on I will attempt my best to answer this question. But know this, it comes down to God granting angels and man both a "free will", which is to say providing them with the ability to choose their own path. God could have certainly created both man and angels to be "robot-like" and to simply love Him so unconditionally that they would say and do everything that God wanted. God is too big and complex for us to fully understand His ways and plans, but suffice it to consider this analogy. If you are a man or woman and you were allowed to create your perfect mate and you could choose whether to allow your mate to love you no matter what, would you choose to make your mate like a robot and love you every day saying it over and over again no matter what you did to them? I think not, as you would quickly become bored as the love exhibited would appear forced and plastic. Since we are created in His image with His likeness, we can more fully understand why God would not want his 'friends" to be "simpletons". God wanted someone, who through the designed likeness of Him, could fully appreciate and love similarly to the way God does. The Lord wanted us to walk and talk with Him and share an appreciation of all things—large and small.

So let us begin to unfold the story of what happened before man appeared on the scene.

CHAPTER 2

Points of Importance

As you read the words that I have written in this book, I want you to remember the following:

1. I will only quote the Holy Scriptures from the Bible. Occasionally I will only reference where in the Bible you may find a corresponding verse that pertains to the subject matter being discussed.

2. I encourage you to use your Bible and read directly from it to make sure I have not taken the liberty to change any of the Holy Scriptures.

3. However, there are many different versions of the Bible— King James, New King James, New International, Holy Trinity, Living Bible, American Standard, New World Translation, etc., so actual words may differ but the "meaning" should be consistent. I also possess a copy

of a New Testament with a word-for-word translation from the original Greek manuscripts, which I may use for word meaning references.

4. I ask that you open your mind and reflect on the information being shared. Pray for discernment.

5. I will at times bold, italicize and/or underline words or statements to assist you in intently considering the importance of the word or group of words.

It is essential that you clearly understand what it means that we are all declared sinners in the sight of God. Sin is by its very nature counter to what the majority, thankfully, believe is the best course of action. Sin is wrongdoing, crime, offense, transgression, error, lapse, misdeed, and many other similar acts.

Let us focus on one sin like crime. We humans have created laws based upon the Ten Commandments handed down to Moses. One law is that it is illegal, based upon morality, to murder someone. I'd say 99% of us agree on the validity of this law. Thus, if someone commits an act of murder, we have come to a consensual agreement in society that a murderer is to be punished.

Well, Jesus points out that one need not even commit a wrongful act to be considered guilty of a sin, and therefore should be punished by God. So that even a person who has ever thought to murder someone in their mind would be guilty of this sin. The same would hold true for stealing, cheating, lying, coveting, false witnessing, etc.

As you can see by this illustration, everyone on the planet has at one time or another committed sin. However, through the grace of God, a person can be forgiven of their sins. The grace of God is nothing more than God's unconditional love shown toward us despite the fact that we are undeserving of His love due to our rebellious nature toward Him.

MOST PEOPLE ARE WILLING TO WORK FOR GOD AS LONG AS THEY ARE HIS ADVISERS.

This grace of God is given freely to those who completely give their body, mind, soul, and spirit to God for His purposes. If one is willing to do this, through the acceptance of His Son Jesus, then you will receive the grace of God. John 1:17 states "For the law was given through Moses, **but God's unfailing love and faithfulness came through Jesus Christ.**" If we accept Jesus then we receive God's grace, which is His unfailing love and faithfulness. The acceptance of Jesus would be you stating before God and publicly the following:

1. Jesus is the Son of God

2. Jesus left His throne in Heaven and took on the form of a man in order to model what your life was meant to be like.

3. Jesus died on the cross of crucifixion in order that His holy blood was used to cleanse the stain of sin from every person.

4. Jesus' death paid the debt, in full, of every person, and that no other amount of "clean" living will add anything to this repayment.

5. Jesus conquered death and sin completely by rising from the dead and is once again on his throne in Heaven.

6. Jesus will return (Second Coming) as promised to finally put all things in order.

Therefore, by stating and believing all of this, you become a disciple of Jesus Christ (Christian).

As a result of Christ's sacrifice, the power of sin is eternally broken and the *presence* of all sin will be removed upon His return, and the ways of this world will be conquered forever!

However, it is important to note that just because you proclaim to be a Christian you will not instantly be transformed outwardly, but rather you will be transformed in spirit. Being a Christian means to "truly" try every waking moment not to sin against others, yourself, or God. In this way, Christianity is a Sin Management Program designed to raise your consciousness to model your life after that of Jesus. To be a Christian means you now desire to proceed in life with the purpose of resembling Jesus—in every aspect of your life.

If you feel as though there must be a "better way" to live your life, then I invite you to pursue your walk with Christ.

CHAPTER 3

Our Beginning

Some will undoubtedly wonder why I have chosen to open this book with a return to an explanation about the "beginning" of time. First of all, it is important to know that "time" is a human discovery if you will. You see God knows no boundary of time. He exists outside of time. **Remember His ways are not your ways.** So immediately dismiss the concept of time as it relates to your Creator.

Also, I believe what I am about to state is paramount in your exploration of Holy Scripture. That is this: If the Bible can't explain where you came from and what happened to mankind, then how can it tell you where you are going and what you need to do to ensure your salvation?

In Colossians 1:15 -16 we are told that *"All things were created by him and for him."* It tells us all things seen and unseen were made by the Creator, and that they serve His purposes. Now with this understanding, we move to the Book of Genesis to explore the story of why we are here and what happened to lead to the predicament in which we now find ourselves.

GOD CREATED US IN HIS LIKENESS.

The book of Genesis starts to tell us about what occurred "In the Beginning". Genesis matters as it is crucial for proving the existence of Christianity, which of course is essential to our redemption. So in Genesis, we learn that God creates the heavens (celestial) and the earth (terrestrial). Please note the heavens are plural, which again I will discuss later in this book, while the earth is singular. The reason the earth is mentioned right away is that God is explaining to Moses that our history, meaning mankind's, begins with the creation of the earth. God created the earth as a garden for his enjoyment and quickly created a gardener (man) to care for the Garden, and ultimately the entire planet. The earth is referred to as God's footstool (Isaiah 66:1). Thus, the earth is important to the Almighty. Obviously, this is a good thing for us!

However, God wants Moses to be able to tell all of mankind that His creation is vast and infinite. God does this in His mentioning the heavens, which is everything else that Moses may look up at and visualize, as well as things he may not be able to see (celestial or spiritual). You can note by reading the first two verses in Genesis that the earth was without shape, void, and there was no sun shining on it as God had not yet created light. God creates the waters, stars, sun, moon, plants, animals, etc. Then on the sixth day He says to his Son Jesus, who has always been with God, "Let US make mankind in OUR image, in our likeness so that they may RULE over the fish in the sea, and the birds in the sky, over livestock and all the wild animals, and over all the creatures that move along the ground." (Genesis1:26)

The important take away is you and every human has been created in the image and likeness of God—so you are indeed very special! Sorry to tell some reading this, but your pets are not special in the way that humans are. Also, God grants us dominion over all living things upon the earth—nothing is our equal on planet earth. God also explains that every other creature or living thing on the planet was just "thought" into being. God then informs Moses that mankind, being so closely resembling God's likeness (sharing attributes of spirituality, morality, and rationality, although imperfectly because of our sin) was actually formed by God from the dirt of the earth (Genesis 2:7). No other creature was formed by God; so God is telling Moses, "You were made to be special to me."

As a result, mankind (man) has a social, mental, and moral likeness to God. We are also special in terms of our physical makeup, but that is not what God meant in stating "in OUR image". I'll explain the uniqueness of our physical makeup in just a short while.

First, we possess a social likeness to God. God has a social nature as displayed by His creation of all things. He clearly desires to create beautiful things and to then interact with them. He provided mankind with this same need for socialization and love. The difference is a man/woman **needs** love/socialization and God merely **wants** love/socialization.

Second, we possess a mental likeness. Man is given abilities far superior to the animals he has been given dominion over. Man is endowed with an intellectual capacity that far exceeds those of animals as he is capable of designing his environment, working with large complex numbers, communicating with each other, and with God. Man possesses a non-instinctive element to his being and as a result he is able to write poetry, appreciate beauty, paint/sculpt, to reason, to laugh at humor and himself, etc. Animals do not possess all or even close to all of these traits.

Third, we possess a moral likeness. Meaning mankind alone has the ability to spiritually commune with God through prayer, praise, and worship. Mankind was conceived as innocent of sin and holy. Only later when we allowed ourselves to be deceived and chose to disobey God did we lose our holiness. At His very essence, God is LOVE! Thus, our likeness to God has everything to do with the fact that we are somewhat similar to God because we can express love for God, people, animals—and even the arts.

God formed each of us through love, and He wants to have a relationship with you! God exhibited his interest in having a relationship with mankind when He revealed Himself to Abraham. He cemented that interest with Moses by choosing to bring Abraham's descendants out of Egypt.

Undoubtedly, Moses wanted to know what happened in the Garden of Eden and why did mankind fall out of favor with God. God of course already knew that Moses would want to know these things so He tells Moses in Genesis 3 that man was kicked out of the Garden because of his failure to obey the instructions/laws of God. Moses learns that a serpent (Satan) deceived mankind by telling Eve that no harm would come to her if she ate the fruit that had been forbidden. In fact, Satan tells her that the only reason God doesn't want her to eat the fruit is because then her eyes would be opened and she would be all knowing like God Himself. She then eats the fruit and convinces her mate Adam to eat it, and they are banished from the Garden for disobeying God's commands (sin). Moses is then filled with understanding that Satan (the fallen angel Lucifer) is an adversary of mankind and that he continues to lie and deceive mankind.

In explaining what Satan has done to mankind, God is informing Moses that Satan is powerful, otherworldly (a talking serpent), and deceptive. In so doing, God has helped

Moses to explain to generations that Satan is a formidable opponent of man and that we are to be ever diligent to not put ourselves in positions that might compromise our ability to ward off his advances.

CHAPTER 4

Before the "Beginning"

So Moses does get some picture that before man was created, a "universe" existed and that our Lord had already not only created the universe as a whole, but He also created some very special spiritual beings called angels. Angels were created to serve God and carry out His commands. Consider Psalm 103:20-21, "Bless the Lord, you **mighty** angels of *his* that carry out *his* orders listening for each of *his* commands. Yes, bless the Lord, you **armies** of *his* angels who **serve** *him* constantly." We see from this passage that God created angels to serve Him and to carry out His orders. Additionally, we learn that the angels are virtually innumerable as they are described as armies— meaning many. In Isaiah 6:1-3, it is revealed to us that there are different types of angels and that they serve different purposes. Consider this, "The year King Uzziah died I saw the Lord! He was sitting on a lofty throne and the Temple was filled with his glory. Hovering about *him* were **mighty**, six-winged angels of fire. With two of their wings, they covered their faces, with two others they covered their feet and with two they flew. In a great antiphonal chorus they sang, "Holy, holy, holy is the Lord Almighty; the whole earth is filled with his glory." Such singing it was! It shook the Temple to its foundations, and suddenly the sanctuary was filled with smoke. As we see the Holy Temple of God is truly amazing and inhabited by his many angels which constantly worship and serve Him.

THE PRINCE OF THIS WORLD DESPISES MANKIND.

Satan, the fallen angel Lucifer, was apparently intent on destroying man's "birthright" to dwell in the Garden of Eden, and ultimately he was successful in doing so. He used his convincing speech to deceive and confuse Eve—who then deceived Adam. I want to make a point here that Eve is no guiltier of sin than Adam. Adam knew better, but he chose, himself, to sin!

God does not reveal to Moses in Genesis where or how Satan came into existence. He simply introduces Satan and tells him that man is to ever be on the lookout for Satan is always looking for an opportunity to destroy man.

In order to learn more about what happened before man existed, we need to go and examine other books in the Bible. We need to now turn to the last book of the Bible—Revelation.

We see in Revelation 12:7-9 "Then there was war in heaven, Michael and the angels under his command fought the Dragon (Satan) and his hosts of **fallen** angels. And the Dragon lost the battle and was *forced* from heaven. This great Dragon—the ancient serpent called the devil, or Satan, the one deceiving the whole world—was thrown down onto the earth with all his army."

This passage is vitally important because these essential elements are revealed:

1. A war broke out in heaven.

2. There were 2 armies of angels fighting against one another. One is obviously loyal to the Almighty God under the command of the archangel Michael, while the other is attempting to overthrow the Most High God and has chosen to follow Lucifer (Satan, the Dragon, Serpent, Deceiver, and many other names used for him).

3. 2/3 of the angels stick with God. 1/3 follow Satan. See Revelation 12:4, however, note that "stars" is a reference to angels.

4. The battle is won by God's army—note it states BATTLE, as the WAR is continuing to this very day!

36

5. Those on the losing side are referred to as "fallen" angels and they are pushed out of heaven, along with their leader Satan, and thrown down to earth to reside there from that point forward. The earth becomes the domain of Satan and his army.

From this, you should now understand that the earth has been "leased" to Satan for he was cast out of heaven and allowed to dwell on earth. Therefore, the world in which we live today and for the foreseeable future is under Satan's power. It was not meant to be this way, as the earth was supposed to be a gift for mankind to have complete dominion. However, at the Garden of Eden, Satan set out to steal man's claim to the earth as well as his "birthright" as a holy creation. We discover in Genesis 3:1-6 that Satan accomplished this by *deceiving* Eve, and she by deceiving Adam. Sin entered the world and man was no longer holy. Satan had pulled mankind down, and he did this out of his jealousy and envy of God. Satan could not stand that man had such a special place with the Creator, and he made it his goal to drive a wedge between man and God. As we know from Scripture, Satan was successful and man was booted out of the garden.

So how could all this be if God created the angels, including Lucifer? Well, remember I had stated previously that God did, in fact, create man, as well as angels. I also noted that God gave both angels and man "free will" and thus the ability to choose their own path of existence. Well, we now know that one angel in heaven, Lucifer, who was the most beautiful and powerful of all the angels created by God, decided he didn't just want to be a powerful angel—he wanted to be God! Isaiah 14:12-17 states this: *"How you are fallen from heaven, O Lucifer, son of the morning! How you are cut down to the ground—**mighty** though you were against the nations of the world, for you said to yourself "I will ascend to heaven and rule the angels. I will take the highest throne. I will preside on the Mount of Assembly far away in the north. I will climb to the highest heavens and be like the Most High." But instead, you will be brought down to the pit of hell, down to its lowest depths. Everyone will stare at you and ask, "Can this be the one who shook the earth and the kingdoms of the world? Can this be the one who destroyed the world and made it into a shambles and demolished its greatest cities and had no mercy on its prisoners?"*

This scripture explains to us again that Lucifer has fallen from heaven because he committed **The First Sin** by trying to assume the position of God. It also shows that he has now become Satan as he wants nothing but the destruction of the world. However, it reassuringly shows that at the end of the war, Satan will be defeated and shown as someone who should never have been feared or revered because his power is temporary - a stark contrast to the power of God!

We further see that Satan suffered from the "I" disease, which is the same disease that many of us humans still suffer from. We are constantly putting ourselves up as better than others and chronically criticizing our fellow man. We begin to show ourselves, just like Lucifer, for our true selves—prideful and jealous. Remember this: Pride always precedes a fall from a lofty position!

Interestingly God appears for a period of time after the battle and His decision to banish Lucifer/Satan to allow Lucifer/Satan to come back to heaven for short visits. Consider Job 1:6-7 and Job 2:1 which says, "One day as the angels came to present themselves before the Lord, Satan, the Accuser, came with them. "Where have you come from?" the Lord asked Satan. And Satan Replied, "From earth, where I've been watching everything that's been going on." In Job 2 it basically says the same thing but it is noted that it is a separate visit.

As you can tell from this passage, which is again God explaining in human terms to Moses, Satan is on earth and he was granted it by God. Furthermore, God is stating that Satan still had/has "visiting" privileges for purposes only known to God. The rest of the conversation between God and Satan regards Satan's desire to do evil things to a righteous man named Job. God allows Satan, which is why he still allows to this day Satan to tempt and "touch" mankind. This would never have been allowed if mankind had obeyed God in the Garden. However, further illumination of this will have to wait for another time. Hopefully, you have learned the important points.

Please note that Lucifer (meaning light bearer) has now become Satan (meaning adversary) after his "fall" from heaven. He, Lucifer, has turned into Satan and has lost his "birthright" to dwell in heaven. God eventually cuts off communication lines with Satan and banishes him to dwell on earth for the remainder of his days.

It is important to recall that angels are not like us—they were always designed to be immortal because of their place in God's plan. They are not formed of the dust of the ground and therefore do not have anything like a human body. They are not able to be destroyed by other angels or man. Angels can only be destroyed by God.

So you may ask what angels are. The word angel means "messenger." Angels, pure spirits, which may with God's permission take on human form, are God's messengers and apparently are given different duties based upon what God desires them to do. It appears the Seraphim angels described in Isaiah 6:3-4 are the highest form of angels as they are the "closest" in proximity to the Heavenly Father, possess six wings, and are in continual acknowledgment of the glory of God. Additionally, in Genesis 3:24 we learn that God places Cherubim angels to guard the entrance of Eden so that mankind may not re-enter the garden. We also know from Exodus 25:18-22 that the Cherubim were used to guard the Ark of the Covenant. Gabriel (Luke 1:26) and Michael (Jude1:9) are noted as Archangels (leaders of angels).However, note that God is explaining to us that He uses angels to send messages to humans. Angels were primarily created to worship God and to carry out duties as assigned to them. Angels are certainly more powerful and intelligent than humans. From scripture (Colossians 1:15-20) we learn that there are angels referred to as, virtues, powers, principalities, dominions and thrones in addition to the seraphim, cherubim, archangels and guardian angels.

Hopefully, this has provided you some knowledge as to what happened before OUR beginning, including the creation of angels. Undoubtedly there may be many more questions in your mind. However, let me remind you again of the all-important statement seen in Isaiah, "My ways are not your ways." You must get this point or ultimately you may drive yourself crazy attempting to understand an infinite God.

CHAPTER 5

Satan and His Spiritual Followers

Please recall what we have learned previously about Lucifer/Satan. Before his banishment from heaven, Lucifer was a "special" angel. Satan was undoubtedly once a Seraphim angel (closest to God) and this is why he is extremely powerful and dangerous. He was adorned with all sorts of precious gemstones and gold—see Ezekiel 28:12-19. Lucifer was meant to "reflect" God's glory and he was put in charge of the other angels. Lucifer became jealous and resentful as he believed he was better than all of the other inhabitants of heaven—including God's Son, Jesus—and yes, even the Heavenly Father Himself. So, in the end, Lucifer's banishment boiled down to his thirst for power and control over all things. Does this sound familiar in our world? It should!

Ezekiel 28:12-19 provides us a detailed description of the beauty, the position in heaven, and the "perfection" with which God blessed his guardian angel, Lucifer. Again God explains what Lucifer did that resulted in his banishment from heaven.

"Son of dust (simply God's way of addressing Ezekiel the prophet) weep for the King of Tyre (another name for Satan). Tell him, the Lord God says: You were the perfection of wisdom and beauty. **You *were in Eden*,** the garden of God; your clothing was bejeweled with every precious stone—ruby, topaz, diamond, chrysolite, onyx, jasper, sapphire, carbuncle and emerald—all in beautiful settings of finest gold. They were given to you on the day you were created. I appointed you to be *the anointed Guardian Angel*. You had access to the holy mountain of God. You walked among the stones of fire (a reference to all the angels)."

"You were perfect in all you did from the day you were created until that time when wrong was found in you. Your great wealth filled you with internal turmoil and you sinned. Therefore, I cast you out of the mountain of God like a common sinner. I destroyed you O Guardian Angel from the midst of the stones of fire. Your heart was filled with **pride** because of all your beauty; you corrupted your wisdom for the sake of your splendor. Therefore, I have cast you down to the ground and exposed you helpless before the curious gaze of kings. You defiled your holiness with lust for gain; therefore I brought forth fire from your own actions and let it burn you to ashes upon the earth in the sight of all those watching you. All who knew you are appalled at your fate; you are an example of horror; you are destroyed forever."

As we can see, Lucifer was appointed by God to be the most special of the guardian angels. He was created more beautiful and wise than all other angels. We learn that Lucifer/Satan was in the Garden of Eden, and had already been on earth as a result of his sinful rebellion against the Almighty. We also see that Satan is already defeated spiritually and that at the "end" he will be mocked by even those who thought he was great; and ultimately, he will be destroyed.

One question for you to ponder is who is the opposite of God? Many will quickly say Satan or the devil. However, this is impossible! An opposite would mean an "equal", and Almighty God has no equal. Lucifer was *created* and can never be equal to God. God has no equal—in the past, in the present, or in the future.

Now back to our investigation of Satan's stranglehold on mankind. Satan apparently becomes further outraged that the Creator decides to create man and to give the earth to his newest creation. As we previously learned, Satan considers the earth his dwelling (after banishment) and isn't about to share it with mankind. He also sees that man has a very special place in God's "eye" since God has created man in his likeness. Thus, Satan sees that man will be as "important" as angels and this does not sit well with him. In fact, God is creating mankind so he has someone to walk and talk with—someone who shares more closely his love of all things. This is the "common likeness" we share with God.

LUCIFER/SATAN WAS CREATED TO BE PERFECT IN EVERY WAY.

In Lucifer's eyes, God has added insult upon his injury. God decides to create man in his own image, and give him dominion over all the earth. Now, this must have enraged an already very unhappy Satan due to the fact that he has set up residence upon and in the earth. Satan must have decided he was not going to lose control of the earth—especially to inferior, weaker creatures like humans. God had expelled him to earth and he was not about to lose his claim to it! Satan obviously hates mankind because we are special in God's eyes, having been created in the *image* of God. God has also given mankind an ability no angel has—procreation! Why can't angels reproduce? Hebrews 12:22 states that innumerable angels were all created at once. Also, angels are immortal, so there is no need for reproduction in God's plan for them. As a result, God apparently decides that all angels will be of the male variety. Scriptures always refer to angels in the male form and use male names exclusively—obviously, this is not the case with humans in Scripture. Since all angels are apparently male, and there are no female angels, reproduction of angels was not in the plan of God.

In Genesis 6:1-6, we are taught that the fallen angels decide to reproduce with beautiful earth women. It does not indicate men ever reproduced with female angels.

"Now a population explosion took place upon the earth. It was at this time that beings of the spirit world looked upon the beautiful earth women and took any they desired to be their wives. Then Jehovah God said, "My Spirit must not forever be disgraced in man, wholly evil as he is. I will give him 120 years to mend his ways." In those days and even **afterwards** when the evil beings from the spirit world were sexually involved with human women, their children became giants (hybrids), of whom so many legends are told. When the Lord God saw the extent of human wickedness, and the trend and direction of man's lives were only towards evil, he was sorry that he had made them. It broke his heart."

It is now revealed to us how significant and truly special the ability to procreate really is in both the terrestrial and celestial worlds. Procreation was something God never intended angels to do—but with Satan's leadership and encouragement, they now had been able to further pollute and "break" the DNA of humans. Therefore, this vile act between these fallen angels and women took us far beyond the original sin of rebellion in the garden, which was the initial "break" in our intended DNA design. Satan had taken God's special creation of mankind and turned it into an abomination. God would not stand for this and did two things: He placed the angels who had done this terrible thing into eternal darkness (see Jude 1:6) and He decided to wipe out all of mankind and the hybrids with a *cleansing flood*. However, his heart finds one righteous man—Noah—who He decides to save along with Noah's family. God does send the flood as we have all heard the story many times. Most of mankind is wiped out; so how is it that giants existed even **afterward?** The answer is not as complex as you might think. Simply the genetics of the hybrids, it appears, continued through the genes of the wives of Noah's sons.

Noah's sons were of the "chosen" genetic tree—they had their roots back to Seth the third born of Adam and Eve. Noah's sons' wives, on the other hand, it appears were from tribes associated with the firstborn of Adam and Eve—Cain. It is quite possible that it was Cain's descendants that had mated with the fallen angels, which would have led to the creation of the hybrid giant superhuman races. So it appears that even after the flood, the corrupted genes survived and were passed along. This is the reason that God in the Old Testament was so instructive to the Israelites to destroy so many of the other races who He deemed to be genetically polluted. Could God have done things in a different way? Sure, but we cannot fully understand His rationale.

Look at what Paul alludes to in Romans 1:18-25 as a view into the possible reasons that the wrath of God was delivered upon these heathen tribes.

"For the wrath of God is revealed from heaven *against all ungodliness and unrighteousness* of men, who suppress the truth in unrighteousness, because what may be **known of God is manifest in them**, for God has shown it to them. For since the creation of the world His **invisible attributes are clearly seen**, being understood by the things that are made, even His eternal power and *Godhead*, so that they are without excuse, because, although they knew God, they did not glorify Him as God, nor were thankful, but became futile in their thoughts, and their foolish hearts were darkened. Professing to be wise, they became fools, and changed the glory of the incorruptible God into an image made like a corruptible man—and birds and four-footed animals and creeping things."

"Therefore God also gave them up to uncleanness, in the lusts of their hearts, to dishonor their bodies among themselves, who *exchanged the truth of God for the lie, and worshipped and served the creature rather than the Creator*—who is blessed forever. Amen."

Despite having firsthand knowledge of God and knowing who He was, these nations filled with people corrupted with tainted DNA chose to follow Satan rather than God. They worshipped images of created animals, committed every type of sexual sin, and their lives were full of every kind of wickedness including murder, crime, envy, hate, greed, etc. In other words, they were continually thinking about new ways of sinning. God did not want his chosen people, the Jews, to be like them—so He ordered the elimination of these nations.

So as we have seen, from what has been presented, Satan comes up with a plan to destroy the "despicable" human creations of God. In order for His plan to work, He must convince "man" to disobey (sin) against God since God cannot be in a relationship with anyone who is unholy. Satan is very smart—beyond the intelligence of man—and he sees that man has also been given "free will", just like he was, and is quite capable of making his own choices. The Bible clearly repeatedly states that our Heavenly Father will not have anything to do with what is unclean, unrighteous, and unholy. So Satan sets his sights on destroying man's relationship with God by getting mankind to sin and to continue to sin against God. Satan chooses to dwell within a serpent to carry out his attack and to deceive the woman, Eve, by telling her a lie about the eating of the fruit of the forbidden tree. Then Eve deceives her mate, Adam, and gets him to eat the forbidden fruit. See Genesis 3.

As a result of all this deception, Satan accomplishes his goal of driving a wedge between God and man which has "somewhat" remained to this day. However, as he always does, Satan underestimates the Creator. God's love for mankind is eternal as evidenced by His decision not to destroy us all in the flood.

Satan obviously miscalculated what God would ultimately decide to do with mankind. Satan was also completely clueless that the Most High God had been preparing to use his Son—Jesus Christ—to put everything back on track.

CHAPTER 6

Jesus—the Savior

There has never been a time when Jesus did not exist. Jesus is of God, and God is of Him. Remember when God said, "let **US** make man in **OUR** image?" To whom was God the Father speaking? The answer is Jesus.

Jesus came to the terrestrial world as the natural Word of God, but in the form of an actual human being. Jesus left his throne in heaven for one purpose—to shed his blood in human death in order to wash away the stain of every human being's sin from the beginning of human history until the end of human history. Jesus was the only acceptable sacrifice God the Father would consider "holy" enough to pay the debt of mankind's sin against God.

Jesus gladly paid the debt demanded. Jesus, who translated means "Jehovah God is with us", left His deity to enter our humanity. He loves each and every one of us so intently that

He left the comfort of heaven and came down to earth to teach us all what it really means to be alive, and of course to die for our sins.

Lucifer knew who the true Son of God was because he had seen Him many times in heaven. He understands that Jesus is superior to him, but he's like the undersized kid we have all known who still thinks he can "take" the big strong kid. I guess once you have gone so far down a path, and even if you are aware that it is the wrong path, you continue to go further because you say to yourself, "the destination can't be that much further." I believe this is the rationale of the Prince of this World!

Did you just say Prince of this World? YES! Read John 12:30-33. Satan is in temporary control of the majority of day-to-day operations on planet earth. He is the one who is the author of disease, pestilence, immorality, hatred, war, and any other undesirable thing. Once Satan was successful in getting man to become sinful, God decided the damage was done and that Satan might as well be used, up until the end times, to determine which people were righteous believers and followers of His Son, Jesus. I strongly urge you to read Revelation 20 & 21. It is important in understanding the future purpose God has in store for Satan. In a nutshell, Satan is first to be bound for 1,000 years while Jesus rules—BUT at the end of the thousand years Satan is to be set free to once again attempt to deceive mankind. If any person is deceived during this time, their fate will be sealed with that of Satan—eternal destruction.

Need more proof that this world belongs to Satan? Undoubtedly you may have heard that Jesus after his baptism by John the Baptist retreated to the desert where He fasted for 40 days and nights. At the end of his fasting who should come along but none other than Satan. Let us read about Jesus being tempted by Satan. Jesus was tempted three times by Satan—but let us focus on one in particular. In Matthew 4:8-11 it is written, "Next Satan took him to the peak of a very high mountain and showed him (Jesus) all the nations and all their glory. "I'll **give it all to you** he said, "If you will only kneel and *worship me.*" "Get out of here, Satan. Jesus told him. "The Scriptures say, "Worship only the Lord God. Obey only him." Then Satan went away and angels came and cared for him."

Note that this passage makes clear who controls the earth and all the nations upon it—Satan. Satan knew that Jesus was the Son of God and that Jesus would not let him stand there promising him falsehoods. Jesus would have called him out by saying something to the effect that you don't own the world! But He didn't do that. Instead, Jesus was listening intently and did nothing to disrespect Satan. Jesus simply was saying no thank you and please leave now.

In addition, Jesus knew that Satan only had a "lease" upon the world. He knew this because his Father had provided

Satan with the "title" of ownership to the earth. Thus, Satan's claim was only temporary—whereas God's claim was, and is, eternal.

JESUS WAS THE ONLY ACCEPTABLE SACRIFICE TO THE FATHER.

Jesus loves you! He will never abandon those whom He loves. All you need do is believe the incredible story before you. You may think the story is impossible—God entering humanity by being born of a virgin peasant girl, being raised by a carpenter, waiting until He was in his 30's to start his ministry, leading a totally sinless existence, performing countless miracles and then willfully allowing Himself to be crucified and to pour out his blood for the purpose of washing away the sins of all of mankind. Improbable—yes. Impossible—NO—this is God's plan.

It will never make total sense in human terms. Remember God telling us "My ways are not your ways." His plans are not what we would even begin to consider. In order for us to accept all of His plans, we must stop trying to put an infinite God in a finite box. We must stop thinking of him as an old man in heaven, or some other made up depiction. Truth is we can't even look upon God's face or we would die! Think of staring at 1 trillion thermo-nuclear bomb blasts simultaneously and believing you wouldn't be blinded and toasted. That's about as close of an analogy as I can get to what it would be like to see God the Father's face. For reference read Exodus 33:18-23 whereby God told Moses that he could not look upon the glory of God's face—that he (Moses) could only view God's back. Ever see the movie Raiders of the Lost Ark? Recall the ending when the Nazis decide to open up the Ark of the Covenant—what comes out from within blows the minds of those looking upon the contents. Again, just a simplistic way for Hollywood to depict the power of the Almighty—but we got the message.

If you are a non-believer and I was to tell you that you would die today—would you not want the opportunity to commune with Christ Jesus eternally, or would you prefer to be non-existent? Ponder that thought.

Jesus states that unless we are like little children we will not see Heaven. What He is saying is that little children accept what their parents tell them as truthful and do not continually second guess their parents. Jesus is saying if you believe in Him and listen to His words, then you will surely have everlasting life.

Therefore, for us to believe that an "impossible" story can actually be not only possible but probable requires one to trust the source—God. However, it is not possible to love someone if you can't trust them. Jesus was asked in Matthew 22:36-40 by a lawyer which of the commandments given to Moses was the greatest. Here is how Jesus replied. "*Love* the Lord your

God with all your heart, soul and mind. This is the first and greatest commandment. The second most important is similar. *Love* your neighbor as much as you love yourself. *All* the other commandments and the demands of the prophets stem from these two laws and are fulfilled **IF** you *OBEY* them. Keep only these and you will find you are obeying all the others." God wants your love above all other things! He also wants you to love your fellow man in such a way that you would only treat another person as if you were treating yourself. A couple of good points here are that you can't love God unless you can treat His Word as holy and needed to assist you in your spiritual walk. In addition, you won't love God unless you first trust Him. Third, you must love yourself, the life given to you, if you, in turn, are to be able to genuinely love others.

God's great expression of love to mankind is the birth, life, death, and resurrection of His Son, Jesus. Your belief in the virgin birth, miracles and ministry, crucifixion, and that Jesus rose from the dead and is once again with His Father in heaven, is all that our wonderful Creator expects from us. So is it not better to have faith in the story of our Savior and be united with God, or to deny that His Son sacrificed Himself for all of mankind? Take a chance and trust me that Jesus is our Lord, Savior and High Priest, and that He is reaching his hand down from heaven to you. Will you be willing to reach upward to grab His hand so that you can commune with God? I certainly hope so!

Remember this: The sin of **omission** (*non-belief*) is without doubt greater than the sin of **co-mission** (*failing to do what we should do*). Jesus wants to be FIRST at all times in your life. Please believe and trust that God's Son did indeed sacrifice Himself to pay off all your sin debts.

CHAPTER 7

Biblical Science

As we delve in a basic discussion here regarding science, it is important to readily admit that the Bible is not a science book. Rather it is a history book, and as a result, it does contain historical science; however, it does not contain in-depth physics, chemistry, biology, etc. Even though, more and more the Bible is found to be as plausible, or more plausible, in its assertions about how the universe and life were formed.

Because of my background in life sciences, I feel adept enough to help define science in a simple way and to explain when something is or is not real science. As a result of my science background, I feel qualified enough to speak on what science consists of and how science has been misused by many to attempt to explain away the Living God and His design of all things. Let's take a look at the word **science**.

Science is a syst
knowledge in the
about the unive
word 'scientia',

Note that sci(
testable/repeat
about the univ
something ca
then it is n
mathematic
readily agreed by scie...
four. We also know that if two hydrogen atoms are
with one oxygen atom it will create water.

before the "big bang", wa
of space. This contradio
(physics), which say
destroyed. Do no
will distort th
been a clo
particle
and

However, much of "science" is not something that can be
duplicated in a lab setting, and therefore it is not real science!
Take for example the theory of evolution. Evolutionary theory
suggests that a "big bang" occurred millions upon millions of
years ago and the universe and the earth were created. When
pressed by someone rational to explain what set off the big
bang, evolutionists are unable to logically explain how the
universe was created. Herein lies the flaw in any evolutionist's
intellectual argument. The question to ask them is, "is it
scientifically possible to create **something** out of **nothing**?"
Of course not! Yet an evolutionist believes that what existed
was a dark space that suddenly burst forth into existence. They
expect you to believe that matter, which didn't exist a second

suddenly created in the vacuum

ts the First Law of Thermodynamics

energy can neither be created nor

be fooled by some highbrow professor who

truth by stating that the universe may not have

ed system or that it could have come from inert

s in a black hole that over a millennia found each other

then created a big bang and the universe sprang forth.

What absolute rubbish!!! Then over many more millions of years these particles became a primordial soup and cells sprang forth, and then similar cells bumped into similar cells making organisms like algae, which clung to rocks and rain fell on them and again many more millions of years went by then fish, amphibians, reptiles, mammals and eventually a human was formed. Really? How can anyone with a rational mind believe this nonsense? Are you aware that the chances of one cell forming randomly, let alone trillions of cells that make up the human body, are so remote that it generally is stated as highly improbable if not impossible?

So let me get this straight, the person who acknowledges that someone (God) who is too complex for our simple minds to totally grasp created all known things is considered "crazy"? While the person who says something can be created from nothing, but then becomes something (particles) and eventually is stirred long enough that a human being is formed is not considered certifiable? What a world indeed. Remember who the father of lies is who deceives the whole world—none other than Satan. He is the one who has the most to gain by convincing man that man is just another set of particles that burst on the scene one day.

In the beginning, God created the heavens and the earth. In this opening sentence in Genesis, we see that God is the Author (energy) of time (beginning), space (heavens), and matter (earth). This is THE basis of physics. It's also the basis of the birth of chemistry. It is estimated that Genesis was written around 1450 B.C.

God explains to us in his Holy Scriptures to have faith that He put all of creation into motion. Look at Hebrews 11:3 "By faith—**by believing God**—we know that the world and the stars—in fact, all things were made at God's *command; and that they were all made from things that can't be seen.*" God is indicating to mankind that He created atoms and their component parts. It wasn't until 1897 that electrons were discovered, thereby proving that atoms had sub-particles. Job 36:26 tells us "God is so great that we cannot begin to know him. No one can begin to understand eternity." The Lord is beyond our human capabilities to **fully** comprehend.

The Bible shows us that God was all over "science" before it was called science. God told the Jews that they should not eat swine. Consider Deuteronomy 14:9 "Pigs may not be eaten....". We learn in the New Testament that we no longer are bound to the law and that all things are from God and therefore are not naturally bad. However, God was providing wisdom noting that swine are not clean animals and therefore more susceptible to parasites. One such roundworm parasite in pigs causes trichinosis in humans. Proper cooking is the only way to kill parasites. God didn't believe mankind was "ready" or diligent enough to cook pork long enough to combat the disease. It took thousands of years to prove why eating pork had risks.

GOD DEMONSTRATES HE CREATED "SCIENCE."

Need more proof of scientific facts attributable to God in the Bible? Consider this:

Genesis 2:7 tells us that God made man from the earth. We now know a man/woman is made up of 28 elements that are found here on our planet.

Leviticus 17:11 introduces mankind to the concept that the life force is in the blood. We didn't begin to understand this until the 16th century. In fact, it was widely thought for centuries that bloodletting was the best way to conquer diseases. Many people died from this approach, including the "father" of our country—George Washington.

Job 26:7 says, "God stretches out heaven over empty space, and **hangs the earth upon nothing."** It wasn't until mankind went out into space in the 1960s that we were able to finally confirm that the earth floated in space suspended upon nothing.

Leviticus chapter 13 speaks of what man is to do in the case of suspected leprosy. It talks about how the high priest is to examine the patient, what they are to look for, quarantining of patients, etc. Early man had no idea about how diseases were spread, and how to protect others from contracting the disease. But God knew, and He shared it with Moses.

In Genesis 6:15, God tells Noah the exact specifications for the building of the Ark so that it would be stable once the flood waters were released. Today shipbuilders know that building a ship that is six times longer in length than it is in width creates good stability—exactly what God told Noah!

Deuteronomy 23:12 states "The toilet area shall be outside the camp." Seems God understood the need for sanitation as well.

Isaiah 40:22 "It is God who sits above the *circle* of the earth. The people below must seem to him like grasshoppers! He is the one who stretches out the heavens like a curtain and makes his tent from them." It is estimated that the book of Isaiah the prophet was written in the 8th century B.C. How did Isaiah know that the earth was spherical in shape? Pythagoras in the 5th century B.C. **proposed** that the earth was not flat. Aristotle didn't confirm that the earth was round/spherical until the 4th century B.C., but he also maintained that all the other planets, as well as the sun, revolved around the earth. Some say it was Eratosthenes in the 3ʳᵈ century B.C. who actually proved the earth was round as he is credited with the discovery of the earth's circumference. I say it was God who told Isaiah at least 300 -500 years before any of the Greeks either proposed or calculated that the earth was round. Furthermore, it was still a popular belief that the earth was flat up until the time of Columbus!

Evolutionists have no explanation for how animals of the same kind would naturally differentiate their reproductive organs, as it would have been necessary for some to evolve as males and some as females at exactly the same time. If not, then the species would not have been able to reproduce further. Genesis 1:27-28 tells us that God made them—male and female. In Genesis 6:19-20 God instructs Noah to bring a male and female of every animal aboard the Ark. It seems God knew and helped identify male and female animals to Noah.

God also states in Genesis 1:24-25 that He brought forth every kind of animal. Thus, it is noted that animals stick to their "kind" for reproductive purposes. Cats breed with other cats and birds with birds. We don't see cats mating with birds.

One mind-boggling item for you to consider is this: It is estimated that the odds that life would form on its own through natural processes outside of a Creator is **1 chance out of 10** to the 40,000 power—that is 1 with 40,000 zeros after the 1! Does life sound like it is the result of a random occurrence?

Human beings have 23 pairs or a total of 46 chromosomes (threadlike nucleic acids in cells that carry our genetic information). So ask yourself this in terms of biological evolution or specialization: Is a human being or a hermit crab more complex? Then why would an evolutionary process create hermit crabs with 254 chromosomes, a fern with 1,260 chromosomes—or even chimpanzees with 48? Additionally, why is it that every other cell in the body, except reproductive cells, contains chromosome pairs? Again, does this sound like a random chance?

There are many more examples of God demonstrating that He is the Author of science. Please just open your bibles and more shall be revealed to you about God and His ways. However, it is imperative that one separate and understand ultimately that there is a difference between a **miraculous event** and a scientifically-quantifiable event. The failure of many is to think that there actually is a scientifically quantifiable explanation for everything in the physical world. There is not! Much of science is a theory—which simply means it a set of conjectures or speculation to explain something. Believers in God's creation have as much or more to stand on than scientists do when it comes to understanding the genesis of the universe and life. It may be mysterious to many, but the more rational person knows in their "being" that it is more plausible that an intelligent architect (God) created the universe and everything in it than to believe all things came from nothing and burst forth on the scene without a catalyst.

It takes considerably more faith to believe in evolution than it does to believe in God as the creator of all things.

CHAPTER 8

New Earth or Old Earth

A prevailing debate between many scientists, mostly physicists, is whether the earth is relatively new—as in thousands of years old, or if the earth is billions of years old. I prayed about this to be revealed to me so that I would know. After all the prayers this is what I believe was stated to my mind.

THE AGE OF THE EARTH SHOULD NOT BE A FOCAL POINT.

The age (time measurement) of the earth should not be the focal point of God's existence or plans. It was previously introduced that God has no need for time—except as a human concept to

67

explain to us, in our diminutive mind capacity, that creation had a "beginning." Thus, creation does not really require time; but that being said, in human terms of time, God could have taken as little or as long as He wanted to create the heavens and the **earth.** So I believe what I've been enlightened to share is that God is saying we have more important things to explore and debate than the age of the earth—that which He will reveal to us one day when He so chooses.

CHAPTER 9

The Three Heavens

I previously noted that God created the **heavens** and the earth. Many read right over Genesis 1:1 and don't give the mention of heavens much thought—thinking heaven is heaven. That's not correct.

There are in fact three distinct heavens. Each heaven has its own purpose and beauty. We will now separate the three.

The first heaven as we look upward is the atmosphere. The atmosphere, which has five layers, is the envelope of gases that surrounds the earth. These gases help keep our planet within the right temperature and humidity, provide air to breathe, etc. The atmosphere, while vaporous, is something we typically think of during daylight when we look up at the blue sky, the bright sun, and the clouds overhead.

The second heaven contains the stars and celestial bodies. This is the celestial or stellar heaven. We recognize it when we look up at night and see the stars twinkling back, the planet Venus brightly shining, or the moon lighting up the night. This heaven is what we think of when we look at the expanse of the universe.

GOD'S "HOME" IS IN THE THIRD HEAVEN.

However, these first two heavens pale in comparison to the splendor of the third heaven, which cannot be seen with the naked eye. This heaven is above the other two heavens and is the place of residence of the Heavenly Father and Jesus Christ. The apostle Paul, in my opinion, gives us the best insight to the third heaven. Look at 2 Corinthians 12:2-4, "Fourteen years ago, I was taken up to heaven for a visit. Don't ask me whether my body was there or just my spirit, for *I don't know; only God can answer that.* But anyway there I was in paradise and heard things so **astounding** that they are beyond a **man's power** to describe or put in words (and anyway *I am not* allowed to tell them to others.)"

Think about what Paul just revealed, albeit in a very limited way. He tells us that he was in paradise and was obviously awestruck with the beauty that surrounded him. He also tells us that he heard things that were utterly amazing—so much so that he couldn't begin to describe it and give it justice. Then he concludes that Jesus told him that he (Paul) was not permitted to speak about it further. Paul has given us just a brief "approved" glimpse of the third heaven. There are many other scriptures about "heaven", but many of the best descriptive ones are in the book of Revelation.

As we see, the Bible, which is a collection of books by authors inspired by God, shows us again how accurate God (Author) is in the words He chooses others to write. He said heavens, not heaven, and He was correct once again.

CHAPTER 10

God/Jesus as Author

Who is this Jesus who only lived 33 years and was just a common man of His times? Some say He was nothing more than a revolutionary rebel, others say He was a lunatic, some said He was the son of the devil, while others describe Him as a "good" man or a prophet. Well, the Bible makes it clear that Jesus is God incarnate—GOD in the flesh! He is God who humbly took on every human characteristic, yet did not sin. Then willfully went to the cross and died to cleanse us of our sins. Yes, Jesus is the loving God who knows and loves everyone of us from the moment we were conceived.

John 1 states, "In the *beginning* was **the Word**, and the Word was with God, and *the Word was God.* He created *everything* there is—*nothing* exists that he didn't make." Jesus is the WORD! Therefore from this scripture, we are clearly informed that Jesus is not only the Son of God—but He is God!

John 1:10-11 further express this point, "But although HE made the world, the world didn't recognize *HIM* when he came. Even in his own land and among his own people, the Jews, he was not accepted."

Jesus never "clearly" stated that He was God (the Father), but He also never clearly denied that He was God. Jesus appears to mankind as a mysterious human being, able to perform astounding miracles, who teaches about God with such conviction that one would be hard- pressed to deny that He had a direct pipeline to the Creator. He is even accused by the Jewish religious leaders of that era, those possibly aligned with Satan rather than God, as the reason for His power to cast out demons. You can read their charge and Jesus' reply in Matthew 12:24-26. Jesus notes that no "house" can stand against itself, implying that if He were of the devil, He would be fighting against Himself, which would be pointless.

After Jesus was resurrected, He appeared numerous times to his disciples. However, one disciple initially was unable to see Jesus—his name was Thomas. Thomas had stated to the other disciples that he would not "believe" Christ had been resurrected unless he could see it for himself. In John 28:24-31 you can read the entire exchange. However, in verse 28, Thomas says, "My Lord and my God!" Jesus makes no attempt to correct him for calling him God, but instead tells him that he believes only because he sees Him. Jesus tells us and anyone who believes in Him and His resurrection without seeing Him that we are even more blessed.

Jesus also shows some mild frustration regarding the disciples' inability to grasp who He truly is. In John 14:8-9, Philip said to Him (Jesus), "Lord show us the Father, and it is sufficient with us." Jesus said to him, "Have I not been with you so long, **and yet you have not known Me, Philip?** He who has seen Me *has seen the Father;* so how can you say, "Show us the *Father"?* Jesus is stating it fairly clear that He is the Father! However, He doesn't say directly that He is the Father. He does this on purpose because He wants them to fully discern this on their own—just like when He provides us the opportunity to choose whether to believe in Him and to love Him. He wants us to trust that He is the great "I Am."

In Exodus 3:13 Moses asks God who should he tell his people is their God's name. God replies, "I AM WHO I AM." Meaning I don't really need a name, but then he does tell us that His name eternally forward is to be Yahweh/Jehovah. When we say, GOD, we are recognizing the "I AM".

Jesus also stated He was "I AM." Consider John 8:58, "I am telling you the truth," Jesus replied. "Before Abraham was born, "I AM." Please note again Jesus could have stated this differently, but He chose to state his reply exactly in this manner. He wants you to see and believe that He is the great "I AM!"

Everything in the Old Testament scriptures is there for one purpose to predict the impending birth, life, death, and resurrection of Jesus Christ. He who is of God and who is God.

JESUS IS GOD INCARNATE.

Jesus of Nazareth was God in the flesh. He chose the right moment in time when all hope seemed to be lost in the world to make His entry into humanity. He did this to save us from our sins. No matter what we do or what we may have done— it would never be enough to pay the wages for our sin. God needed mankind to have an opportunity to once again walk and talk with him. Enter Jesus who took all the sins of all of mankind upon Him to be washed clean by His sacrificial blood. Jesus obviously never sinned during His human lifetime, and He left us with a model on how to live our lives. Jesus also said that any man who believed in Him would have everlasting life. Don't lose your opportunity for this due to pride, resentment, or because you find the story of him improbable.

There are many scriptures that tell us about the coming of Jesus. To me, the most telling one is Micah which was written 700 years before Jesus birth. Micah says in 5:2, "O, Bethlehem Ephrathah, you are but a small Judean village, yet you will be the birthplace of my King who is alive from everlasting ages past! God will abandon his people to his enemies *until* she who is to give birth has her son; ..." Isaiah 53 says many things about the Messiah and is worth reading in its entirety so you can see with clarity that Jesus was the Messiah that was to redeem the world. Just look at Isaiah 53:5-6, "But he was wounded and bruised for our sins. He was beaten so that we might have peace; he was lashed—and we were healed! *We*—everyone of us—have strayed away like sheep! *We*, **who left God's paths to follow our own.** Yet God laid on **him the guilt and sins of every one of us!**" Again, this was also written over 700 years before Christ was born.

God, Jesus, was providing all the clues to His arrival on planet earth in the form of a human child. Most Jews of the time it appears were unable to put all the pieces together to be able to recognize that Jesus was the Messiah, the Savior of the world, and missed out on seeing God in the flesh. Isaiah 9:6 "For to us (Jews) a child is born, to us a *son* is given, and the government will be on his shoulders. And he will be called Wonderful Counselor, **Mighty God, Everlasting Father,** and Prince of Peace." This is utterly amazing that a human being would be referred to as "Mighty God" and "Everlasting Father". These titles were reserved only for GOD Himself. Isaiah states plainly that these will be among the things that this boy child will be called is truly otherworldly in nature.

Why some things God reveals are easily understood and others are so darn difficult, mysterious or humanly improbable is something that frustrates and bewilders us. I don't have all the answers as to the "why" God chose one way over another. Frankly, they are way beyond my abilities. I'm just trying to give you glimpses of His awesome ways and plans. Only He knows what all the plans look like.

CHAPTER 11

Infinite Compassion

God entered the world through the birth of a child—Jesus. Jesus came to experience fully in the flesh what it was to be a man, to teach us about the Father and His desire for us to have fulfilling lives, to take all the sin of the world upon Him to the cross and to die for our salvation, and then to conquer even physical death through his resurrection.

Many who do not know Christ Jesus fully ask things like:

> *"Why would God come down from heaven and be born as a child?"*
>
> *"How could God be in a human for 33 years and be ruling the universe at the same time?"*
>
> *"Why does Jesus refer to Himself as the Son of Man and not God?"*
>
> *"Why does Jesus pray to the "Father" in the garden if He is the Father?"*

Let me feebly attempt a little story here that I hope somewhat parallels.

Once upon a time, a great and powerful king ruled over all that was seen or could be imagined by his subjects. He obviously could have anything he desired as no one questioned his authority. One day he decided to disguise himself and go to town to see what went on—like most times when he visited everyone stopped what they were doing and paid deference to him. Thus, he never really saw how most folks acted and behaved.

He was shocked to discover on his visit that many of the people he thought were "good" were in fact really "bad". Likewise, many he had viewed as "bad" were hardworking and kind people.

As he strolled he came upon a young peasant lady who was absolutely gorgeous. He was instantly enamored with her but did not want to reveal that he was her king for fear she might only visit him out of obligation. However, he decided he wanted to know her better. He learned all he could about her, like the village she lived in, her job, favorite food, etc.—all of which to give him more of a chance with her.

He then decided one day to bump into her in the park while disguised. He talked to her some and asked her inquiring questions. While she thought of him as nice and respectful she was not overly impressed. He decided to keep this up for a while to see if she would warm up to him. Soon she began to see that he was smart and compassionate.

Upon their third encounter she thought to herself he resembles the king in some ways. She told him that he resembled the king, and he quickly deflected the comparison. However, she went on that the king was a good person and that he cared for and protected his subjects—and that one day she would like to meet him and tell him. In his heart, he was very upbeat to hear her thoughts about him.

Unfortunately, before their next visit to the park, her father promised her to another man as was the custom of their nation. When the king ran into her again she said she was engaged to be married and that she could no longer speak to other men as it would not be right. The king was heartbroken—he had missed his chance to win her heart.

The lady got married and was building her life with her new husband. One day her husband decided to steal from a wealthy lord, the king's cousin. Stealing in the nation carried a hefty punishment. If married, the wife was to also receive punishment as she was considered guilty by association. One day the king again went to the town and saw the woman for whom he had love and she was walking toward the park. He followed her and saw her sit on a park bench and she began to cry. He was distraught watching her cry from a distance so he finally approached her and she told him that her husband had stolen from the lord (king's cousin) because they were desperate for food and had no money to use. She then said that the judge had just issued his punishment and she had to go back before the judge in a month with an exorbitant amount of cash for restitution or that she would be imprisoned. The king was moved by her honesty and the situation.

A month passed by quickly and the woman was brought back to court for her final sentencing. The judge asked if she had the money to essentially pay for her continued freedom. She bowed her head and said to the judge that she could not come up with that much money. The judge was about to proclaim the sentence on her of imprisonment when suddenly someone shouted: "I will pay her debt." It was the king, but he was in disguise. The judge said, "This is not permitted within the law!" "On whose authority is it not permitted?" asked the disguised king. "By the King's authority" stated the judge.

As the woman stood unbelieving that someone else she only partly knew was willing to pay the exorbitant debt for her; the king pondered whether to reveal himself. He then knew he had no choice. He took off his disguise, the crowd in the courtroom gasped and fell to their knees, and the judge immediately bowed and said: "Sire if I had known it was you I would..." The woman was in disbelief that the stranger for whom she had "loved" was really the king and that he was standing in her place to pay her debts.

The King told the court that "This judge has ruled wisely and interpreted the law fairly. However, our law needs to allow others to choose to stand in for another if they so choose to do so. Today I choose to take upon me all the debts of this woman as required by our law."

WE OWED A DEBT WE COULDN'T PAY. JESUS PAID A DEBT HE DID NOT OWE.

So this King chose to take her debts and pay for them himself. This is also the story of Jesus. Jesus, our God partially disguised, took all of our debts (sins) upon him at Golgotha/Calvary, and He gladly paid those debts in full. He was beaten, He was whipped unmercifully, and He was stripped of his outer robes. He was mocked and spit upon by his condemners and forced to wear a crown of thorns that was pressed into the flesh of his head and brow. He was forced to carry his own instrument of death—His cross. He was then nailed to that cross in His battered and bleeding condition right next to common criminals. He was jeered at by even some of those who had previously thought of him as a great prophet, all the while struggling with each passing breath as suffocation set in on his physical body. Undoubtedly, He could visualize Satan laughing at him hanging upon the cross, while demons surrounded Him goading him to remove Himself from the cross if He was indeed the Son of God. He refused to come down and He refused to blame others for his predicament; instead, He prayed for their salvation.

Should anyone ever ask you who killed Jesus Christ—without hesitation say, "I did!" Your sins, as well as all of mine, and every sin of every other human being were placed upon Jesus at the crucifixion. He died so that we could be saved. He bled so that we might be cleansed.

Thank you, Jesus, for loving me so much that you died for me.

CHAPTER 12

The War Continues Today

Even for us as Christians, humanly it is normal for us to want more as we move through life, but spiritually we innately realize we actually need less. The only reason this is possible is that we are filled up with Jesus. When Jesus does not fill us up, even temporarily, a void is created and this is when we are vulnerable to the words and deceptions from the evil spirits that are constantly hovering around us awaiting an opportunity to strike.

A spiritual war is happening around us all the time. Satan and his demons continue to fight over our minds. Why? Because the human mind is special! We are reminded that our minds are capable of creating fine art, making beautiful music, solving complex problems, saving lives, and many other wondrous activities. We know that Satan is attempting to prove to God that his creation of man is not special and that we are lowly animals which should be exterminated. As we also know, the Evil One uses many tactics against humanity to deceive and control.

To avoid being another casualty/fatality in this ongoing war, it is essential that we fill ourselves up with Jesus via the words of the Bible. We are to trust in the one who has all the answers—that is Jesus! We know that as Christians we are no better in worldly measurements than those of other beliefs—but that we are better off spiritually because we know that Jesus is the only way to redemption.

We know we are to choose love over hate, and that we are to show it and say it daily. This is what Christ Jesus modeled for us. To not do it would be disobeying His teachings.

SATAN'S GREATEST DECEPTION
IS CONVINCING MOST PEOPLE
THAT HE IS NOT "REAL."

Unfortunately, many believers routinely fail to express or demonstrate their love for others on a daily basis. Again, one reason is they get caught up in the "world" and its ways rather than God's ways. Even Christians allow themselves to create voids in their minds and quickly learn that evil stands ever ready to move in and occupy the void. When evil moves in we begin to be self-centered in our planning. Soon thereafter we begin to note declines in our spirituality, emotional connections, physical and mental health, and/or our financial well-being. Everyday life begins to take its toll on our very existence. We feel empty, unsatisfied, or jealousy, and envy creep into our thoughts. We then seek out activities to excite or satisfy our desires. As we obtain more, and thus feel more in control/power, we desire even more and more to satisfy our urges and desires. We can become overly-proud of worldly accomplishments and begin to believe everything we do must be destined. Well, guess who all of that sounds like? Yes— Satan.

He stands ready to pull you down in the mud of sin. Will you allow him to do so?

Equality is Lost

When the Lord created man, then woman, He created mankind. Eve was created from Adam—specifically the rib of Adam. Why did God do this? The answer is clear from Jesus' statement in Matthew 19:5, *"For this reason a man will leave his father and mother and be united to his wife and the two will become one flesh?"*

Jesus is tying back to what Adam said when he was presented with Eve in Genesis 2:21-24.

"And the Lord God caused a deep sleep to fall on Adam, and he slept; and he took one of his ribs, and closed up the flesh in its place. Then the rib which the Lord God had taken from man He made into a woman, and he brought her to the man. And Adam said:

"This is now bone of my bones and flesh of my flesh; She shall be called Woman for she was taken out of man."

"Therefore a man shall leave his father and mother and be joined to his wife, and they shall become one flesh."

Are you not blown away that Jesus quoted verbatim what Adam said in the Garden of Eden?

Thus, Jesus is making sure that mankind sees what He had intended from the beginning. That man and woman are of one flesh. Now ask yourself can most of us bring ourselves to harm our own flesh? Obviously, the answer is NO—barring some type of mental instability.

This is an extremely important point. God never intended anything but the equality of men and women. He created them from one flesh (bone). The woman was taken out of man only because the man was created first—but it was always the plan that they would realize "inside" that they needed one another to "complete" them spiritually. Soul mates for sure.

So what happened to this original plan of equality? What caused men to dominate the world for so long in our history?

The answers to these and some other interesting questions are contained in Genesis 3. In order to understand what happened in the Garden of Eden and the results of the fall of mankind, you will need to read the entire chapter, probably several times.

The following is an overview in a fairly basic description:

We know that Adam, not Eve, was told not to eat from the tree of conscience (good & evil).

However, we can presume since Adam was the original gardener that he explained to Eve, after her creation, that they were not to eat from the tree of conscience.

We are told that a **serpent** (Satan manifests within) was the most *cunning* of all the beasts created. Cunning means to be skillful at deceit!

Snakes at one time most likely had legs—we know this from examining the skeletons of snakes. Thus, it is "possible" the serpent may have had legs.

We know the serpent was able to speak as it is obvious from Scripture that it conversed with Eve.

We see no sign of Eve being repulsed by the sight of the serpent or anything noting that she was surprised that it could speak. This could simply be due to her innocence since the fall had not taken place yet.

However, we do know that from Ezekiel 28:12-19, previously presented, that God clearly references that Lucifer/Satan was in Eden.

Revelation 12:9, "This great Dragon—the *ancient serpent called the devil,* or Satan, the one **deceiving** the whole world (*present and past tense*) - was (past tense) thrown down to the earth." So we know from this description that Lucifer/Satan was cast down from heaven to the earth for his disobedience and that he has dwelled here ever since and that he has been misleading all of mankind since the Garden of Eden.

Satan first demonstrates his power of deception in the garden by asking or saying things with subtle half-truths. Satan then is able to easily manipulate a vastly inferior mind. Satan asks Eve in such a way that he just appears to be requesting information rather than pouncing and presenting that God is a liar, which he realizes would have been alarming to her. Instead, he poses a question. Basically, the question from Satan goes like this: So let me get this straight. You are not to eat from any of the fruit in the garden? To which Eve replies with dismay—Well, of course, we can eat the fruit you dummy. We just can't eat fruit from the tree at the center of the garden, nor can we even touch it or we will die! Unfortunately, Eve is distorting what God had told Adam—probably due to nothing more than not paying attention to exactly the words of God. God did not tell Adam that if they *touched* the fruit they would die. Obviously, this inattention to God's Word continues to this very day and has grave consequences for man.

This is all the opening Satan needs, as he had heard what God had said to Adam. He tells Eve that God has told them incorrectly and that they will not die—in fact, the only reason God does not want them to eat the fruit from that tree is that *their eyes will be opened* and they will become as powerful and all-knowing as God. Eve states that the fruit's appearance is beautiful and eating it would make her very wise. The hook is set and she takes a bite and apparently convinces Adam to do so as well. They instantly become aware of their nakedness— sin has entered the world.

God comes calling them, knowing what they have done and expresses His displeasure. He talks to all three participants and punishes all of them in a very personal and unique way. The serpent as the vessel of Satan is cursed to never walk on legs again. Satan is told that he and the woman's seeds shall forever be enemies, and that one day one of her seeds will come to crush him. Eve (representative of all women) is to now have children in considerable pain. Also, she is to be more sensitive than a man as she will have increased sorrow to things that happen to her and around her. The final curse on Eve is that she will now lose her equal standing with men (Adam) as he will become her master, and yet she will welcome his affections!

As a result of the "fall", women paid a heavy price. God has told us in His commandments that there are to be no others before Him in our lives. However, this was innate with Eve— but she put herself before God anyway. **Her choice to place herself on par with God is the same sinful act that Satan had committed in Heaven that led to his banishment to**

the earth. Eve shows herself to be idolatrous—wanting to make herself as "like God, knowing good and evil" as was explained to her by Satan. Note what is said in Genesis 3:6, "So when the woman saw that the tree was good for food, that it was pleasant to the eyes, and a tree desirable to make one wise, she took its fruit and ate. She also gave to her husband with her, and he ate." Eve is justifying her decision to eat the fruit and become as wise as God. She then also talks her husband into committing the same sin—I guess we can say he was blinded by his love—for it was dumb. This verse makes the point that woman (women) may be more apt to be influenced toward idolatry, as it was the woman, not the man, who Satan targeted. So when God places His punishment upon Eve, He is saying that women from this point forward, as a general rule, will now need men to replace the spiritual and emotional connection that He is withdrawing from them as a result of the sin. He is also making it clear that, as a result, relational discord will be the norm from this day forward.

However, man does not get a free pass either. Adam was first and he was to lead and protect his wife and he failed to do so. As a result of his sin, he must now be a master—with all the problems associated with being in charge, whereas before he and Eve would have shared in all things equally—including leadership. Also, since man came from the earth/ground, God places a curse on the ground and makes it clear to Adam that he will be banned from Eden and that from now on he will have to "farm" the soil to provide food, and that the curse will make it increasingly difficult to tame the land. Furthermore, it appears as though God decided to change some animals now to be carnivorous, so man has to run and hide from some animals lest they eat him for dinner. While this is not stated in Genesis 3, it is a common observation today that some animals do eat the flesh of other animals. Prior to the "fall", it would appear that the animals were not interested in Adam as a food item as all were brought forth before him to be named.

Sin changed it all! All because we live to satisfy ourselves rather than the Creator who created us **for His pleasure**. We didn't create God.

One final concept to introduce here is the fact that God has clearly created instruments to test man in order to determine if he will be lovingly obedient. To me, God is saying that He put two trees at the center of the Garden of Eden. One is the Tree of Good & Evil (conscience), which is representative of our adversary Satan and his broken world of death and destruction. Unfortunately, this tree clearly wowed Eve with the beauty of its fruit—which was only a deception.

The other tree is the Tree of Life (immortality), which represents Jesus. Its fruit and overall appearance may not have been nearly as attractive as the Tree of Conscience. However, its fruit was eternally sustaining to the soul, the real life force of man.

In other words, God has been testing man since He created them. He wanted us to love, respect, and obey Him just as a child chooses to love and respect their earthly father. Instead, man chose to love himself ahead of God by his willingness to disobey and sin; and he continues to put himself in front of God. It will not end until the return of Jesus is witnessed.

We need to know that from the beginning of time, God created man and woman to be coequal. However, God had no intention of a man and woman being the "same". Satan is the one who is tearing at the very fabric of humanity by continually pushing his agenda to convince us that a man and woman should be the same. Look around and you see culture attempting to influence us that men and women should be "exactly" alike. This was never God's intention as He created us to be equal to one another but to possess attributes that complement the other gender.

FROM THE BEGINNING OF TIME, GOD CREATED MAN AND WOMAN TO BE COEQUAL.

Many people who read Scripture mistakenly interpret some passages when it comes to the equality issue. For example, some read one word or two and then overemphasize what is actually being said. Ephesians 5:23-33 is one such section of Scripture that many feminist leaning individuals will want to argue about contending that women are shown to be "inferior" to men. Let's examine the verses together and then unpack their true meaning.

"Wives, **submit** to your own husbands, as to the Lord. For the husband is the **head** of the wife, as also Christ is head of the church; and He is the Savior of the body. Therefore, just as the church is **subject** to Christ, so let the wives be to their own husbands in everything. Husbands, love your wives, just as Christ loved the church and **gave himself for her, that He** might sanctify and cleanse her with the washing of water by the word, that He might present her to Himself a glorious church, not having spot or wrinkle or any such thing, but that she should be holy and without blemish. So husbands ought to love their own wives as their own bodies; he who loves his wife loves himself. For no one ever hated his own flesh, but nourishes and cherishes it, just as the Lord does the church. For we are members of His body, of His flesh and of His bones. For this reason, a man shall leave his father and mother and be joined to his wife, and the two shall become one flesh. This is a great mystery, but I speak concerning Christ and the church. Nevertheless let each one of you in particular so love his own wife as himself, and let the wife see that she respects her husband."

So you see if one only read the first part of the message, one could overemphasize the words submit, head, and subject, thereby reading into this message that a woman is inferior because it is telling her to submit to her husband as he rules over her as if she is his subject. Nothing could be further from the truth when you read the entire message. God is simply talking about the path to a good marriage. He is noting that men, in particular, like to be respected and admired, and that a loving wife will provide him with that. You see, submitting can be done either willingly or unwillingly. You have been led to believe it is only an unwilling act. If I know my wife strongly desires something of me and I willingly want her to have that something from me, does that mean that I was coerced? Of course not! In fact, the other verses quoted show plainly that a man is to care for his wife as if she is his own flesh. Most of us do not do things to harm our own bodies purposely. God is telling husbands to love their wives as much as they love themselves.

Examine the following as evidence to consider in determining true superiority. Ask yourself if a diamond is superior to bread? No, it is not superior, and bread is not superior to a diamond. What is deemed to be superior depends upon the moment in time and the task at hand. If I am hungry, a diamond will not do me much good. Likewise, if I wanted to cut glass, a piece of bread would be worthless. This is the way it is with a man and a woman. Generally speaking, we know that a man has more muscle, broader shoulders, runs faster, has more coarse features and is more likely to gravitate toward facts and logic in his thinking. Again, generally, women have less muscle, broader hips, run slower, have more delicate beautiful features and gravitate toward emotion and intuition in information processing. Thus, if one is looking upon a fine painting of a scene depicting a couple fishermen and their small boat, the woman might describe the painting as having a wonderful depth and texture that captures the expressive love that the artist must have felt in that moment. The man next to her might say it's a nice painting of two fishermen with a dilapidated boat, a net full of holes, and therefore it's no wonder they didn't catch any fish!

Was either of them superior or inferior in their interpretation of the painting? No, they see the painting from different points of view. This is the way each of them—man and woman—were generally designed by the Creator. In this way, they complement each other's skill sets and fully put into perspective the complete interpretation of the painting.

We must celebrate and embrace our gender differences, noting that from time-to-time an exception to the general rule may be observed. This does not mean that we throw out the general consensus, nor should we judge a couple where the woman is physically stronger to the man in the relationship, or the man who is more prone to emotion than his wife. It does not matter to God as long as they are in agreement with their roles. God has helped them to find mates that fulfill their specific needs.

The headship reference above from Ephesians is also stated in 1 Corinthians 11:3, "But I want you to know that the head of every man is Christ, the head of a woman is man, and the head of Christ is God." This is simply declaring an order of leadership. This is stating from God's perspective a man is to be the leader/master within his family unit. Does this mean that the woman can never take responsibility to lead the family? No, not at all. It is stating that when an issue does face the family, that the man will ultimately be expected to resolve the issue for the family. Man is put into the position of responsibility and authority as a result of his failure in the Garden of Eden. In fact, by examining Romans 5:12 we see from God's perspective that sin entered the world through Adam, not Eve. God holds Adam accountable for not being vigilant about Eve's whereabouts in the Garden, for had he been with her when Satan approached he would have been able to rebuke him. Thus, Adam's failure to protect Eve produced the opportunity for sin to enter the world.

Also please note that a man's head is Christ, and God is the head of Christ. Thus, responsibility and accountability have a specific order.

Do not let yourself be misled by the evil one who is constantly attempting to drive a wedge between man and woman—and also man and God. Discord is what Satan preaches.

CHAPTER 14

The Triune (Trinity) Nature of God

Many people, including myself at one time, find it challenging to understand the triune nature of the Creator. One can quickly point to the fact that the Bible does not even contain the word Trinity within its pages. So how is it possible that God would have three persons (entities) contained within the Godhead?

The issue of understanding this concept is to first dismiss "worldly" logic. If you attempt to explain the Trinity of God in physical worldly ways, you will find it virtually impossible. Instead, you must open up to the Holy Spirit within you to help you understand. In other words, logic must be put aside and you must rely on your spirituality to guide you.

The problem of not being able to accept that God has three "Persons" is somewhat understandable, as it defies human logic. There are no parallels contained within our physical world. So to fully understand the Godhead (Trinity), you must first remind yourself that God's ways are not your ways! It is important that you dismiss what you have always been told; that two things cannot occupy the same space. This is a widely accepted truth in the physical human world—so it makes perfect sense for a person to find it difficult to view that God the Father, Jesus, and the Holy Spirit can all be within one. However, the Bible makes it clear that two or more objects in the **unseen spiritual world** absolutely may occupy the same space. We then can see that many things in the unseen spiritual world have different laws of time, space, and matter.

I once was guilty of not allowing the Holy Spirit to guide me in this regard. I used my knowledge of science and human logic as my defense that the Bible was telling me that God the Father, Jesus, and the Holy Ghost were all separate entities, rather than expressions of the same God. I would point to the fact that Jesus called himself the Son of Man. Jesus never said "directly" that He was God. I reasoned, why would God want to make all this so complicated. I showed my spiritual immaturity in those days. I failed to recall the simple point that Jesus seemed to always speak in parables. In fact, Jesus was questioned by his disciples in Matthew 13:10 as to why He spoke in such hard to understand ways. Let us read the scripture verse, "His disciples came and asked him, Why do you use these hard to understand illustrations?"

In Matthew 13:11-13 we learn what Jesus' response was, "Then he explained to them that only they (Disciples of Christ) were *permitted* to understand about the Kingdom of Heaven, and others were not." "For he that has more will be given…"

Jesus makes it clear that He is purposely making his message "difficult" to decipher—for a reason known to Him. He is also noting that only those who choose to actively seek his message, in His Word the Bible, will ever be able to comprehend. Jesus is saying that if a person, even one who calls himself a disciple of Jesus, does not regularly read His Word and seek Him continually on their own accord, rather than relying on a pastor or priest to tell them the Word of the Bible, then even what they thought they knew would be slowly eroded from their minds. It appears that spiritual laziness will not be tolerated by the Lord! Yet many show up to churches every week with the expectation that listening to their priest or pastor will suffice them until the following week. And they repeat this pattern over and over again.

As I stated earlier, I was told my laziness would no longer be tolerated. God informed me that a special ability to explain His Word was provided to me for His purposes and that it was no longer going to be acceptable for me to ignore His call to use this ability. Of course, you are welcome to believe whatever you want to about me—but know this; His will be done. Deny Him what He desires of you, and you will pay a price.

I'll also quickly clarify what I have said previously about not having any formal teaching in theology. I need to amend that to say I have no teaching in this physical world—but rather my teaching comes from Jesus himself through the Holy Spirit who explains to me what it is that I am reading. What teacher is more credentialed than Christ? Thus, I believe I have learned from the very best teacher—Jesus.

Now let us return to Scripture to learn that indeed two or more things can occupy the same space. For this, we turn to read a story in Matthew 17:14-21. You should read it for yourself, but here is the main theme. A young boy is possessed by a demon that is so strong the apostles are unable to cast (exorcize) the demon out. Here is the reason for visiting these scriptures. If a demon is within a person—then is it not occupying the same space as the person, in this case the boy? Did a light bulb just turn on in your mind? It should have.

So ask yourself if it is possible for a demon to occupy the same space as a person, wouldn't it be easy for God to be occupying spaces simultaneously. Of course it would!

These points were my stumbling points until Jesus enlightened me. I can only hope I have helped you to understand this so you won't continue to stumble over the Trinity.

So when someone says to you, "Okay if Jesus is God—then how was it that God was born as a human baby? Who was ruling the universe while God was dwelling in Jesus?" This demonstrates the spiritual immaturity that many possess— some much longer than others. Obviously, God can express Himself in any way or within any form. His plans are not the plans you would choose. So it is time that you let go of any "logic" that is preventing you from feeling the way the Holy Spirit would have you go.

TO FULLY UNDERSTAND THE GODHEAD/ TRINITY YOU MUST REMIND YOURSELF THAT GOD'S WAYS ARE NOT YOUR WAYS.

So hopefully we can agree that in the spirit world it is possible for two entities to occupy the same space. So it is not a big leap to understanding that God can also be in more than one place at a time. While in the human form God never relinquished his control of the entire universe. God the Father, Jesus the Son of God and the Holy Spirit are the three persons expressed by God. Each has its own uniqueness and purpose. God uses these different manifestations to help guide us in our walk with him. The Father is Creator; Jesus is the Word and teacher, while the Holy Spirit is our daily comforter and guide in our walk. Open your mind and your heart and the Spirit of God will lead you to know him more intimately.

Are you still in need of some further evidence? First, look to how things even in our natural world have a "triune" nature—meaning things that can exist in three states of matter. Take water for instance—good old H2O. Water can exist in three states—as a solid (ice), liquid (water), and as a gas/vapor (steam/cloud). However, they are all the same in chemical structure! All three states are still H2O. No one typically says that water and ice are two different entities. Yet, if you mention that God exists in three "persons"—Father, Son, and Holy Spirit some will inevitably say that is impossible! Really? Again, your mind is closed to the obvious.

In fact, most chemical elements can exist as solids, liquids, and gases—under the right set of conditions (temperature, pressure). Mercury is one element that can readily be understood by most folks as having three states of matter.

There are also many scripture verses that should lead one to "see" the triune nature of God. Open your Bible and read Matthew 28:19 where Jesus says, "Go therefore and make disciples of all the nations, baptizing them in the name **of the Father and of the Son and of the Holy Spirit.**" Jesus could have said "Go therefore and baptize them in the name of God (Yahweh)," but He didn't. Jesus is clearly noting the nature of God as one—but consisting of three distinct parts. The three are a team.

While there are many scriptures that demonstrate the triune nature of Almighty God, here is one more I find to be most convincing. Consider 1 John 5:7 which states, *"For there are three that bear witness in heaven: the Father, the Word (Jesus) and the Holy Spirit; and these three are one."* (Please make special note that this is what the NKJV says verbatim, and the KJV is the same except for linguistic changes to old English. However, the NIV and NLT simply say this—"For there are three that testify." This is an important point that I only alluded to earlier. Some translations have been modified from the original language. This is clearly an example of why one must be "cautious" in reading some translations. Remember our adversary is always working upon the mind to create confusion, doubt, etc. in our minds. Again, pray that the Holy Spirit guide you, read things for yourself, and examine many versions before settling on what you perceive to be correct.

My final verse for demonstrating the triune nature of God comes from John 20:26-29, but specifically the 28th verse. This is where "doubting" Thomas who has refused to believe in the resurrection of Jesus—is confronted by Jesus and is asked if he now believes. Please note what Thomas says now that he believes Christ has risen. "Thomas said to him (Jesus), "My Lord and my God." Thomas has just called Jesus God! The more interesting part is that Jesus makes no attempt to correct him.

At the end of the day, the concept of the Trinity is a complex one that will require much searching on your part. The only way you will fully understand God's triune nature is to pray and ask God for his revealing. No amount of science, logic, philosophy or any other human way will ever be able to "prove" it to you.

So can one be a "believer" but not believe in the Trinity? You can be a believer, but you will believe in something other than what God seems to want us to believe. A better question is can one be saved and not believe in the Trinity? Jesus said with God all things are possible—so it is not a man's place to say, for God will choose to save whom He chooses. Of course, He promises to save ALL those who believe in his Son, Jesus.

CHAPTER 15

Failure is Not Final

The great thing about God is He gives 2nd, 3rd, 4th........ chances to those He loves—all of mankind. We again think within a three-dimensional world, and as a result, tend to think of our decisions and actions as being final. Thus, we say we committed a sin and there is "no way God can forgive me." Well, fortunately, He will forgive you by your believing in His Son, Jesus Christ, who is Lord and Savior– but He may punish you first. The punishment delved out is "just" since it has been determined by God. Many of us want to discuss the punishment with God—plead our case so to speak. Save the speech as God has already heard it all.

However is it not unbelievable how even when we fail, that God has a plan to restore us? God has never asked us for more than what we are capable of doing. He has always asked us to simply trust Him and to obey Him. Yet, the majority of us do not trust Him enough to obey Him. We continue in the same pattern of disobedience that Adam and Eve exhibited—which is basically idolatry as man continues to want to place himself in a position of authority as high as God. We chose to follow Satan's plan rather than God's and we have been paying a very high price ever since.

Thankfully, God has never given up on his special creation—mankind. As a result, He has not, nor will He ever, give up on YOU! Many people are tricked into believing the lies that are whispered to them from Satan. Satan tells them to remember this sin or that sin you committed, and that as a result God has turned his back and given up on you. The words Satan whispers and the feelings that he causes to be brought back to the surface wear on us. We begin to feel totally inadequate and that Satan must be right; that there is no way Jesus could possibly love us enough to forgive us for the horrendous things we have done.

Satan is the father of lies and will constantly stand against you. He is like a prosecuting attorney in court (your mind) who bases his whole case against you on fabrications, distortions, and on old news (sins) for which the fine has been paid by Jesus. Satan is most persuasive in convincing many that Jesus does not and will not forgive you of the sins that you have already confessed. This is an absolute lie! Your sin debt for every sin you have committed—or will commit—have been paid in full by the blood of Jesus Christ upon the cross—provided you believe in

Jesus as your Lord and Savior, and that you repent of your sins in a genuine fashion. By doing this you acknowledge that the grace of Jesus is wholly sufficient for you.

Please realize that God has, throughout the Bible, chosen to work his plans through those we would never expect that He would have designated. Consider Moses, a man who murdered a man, ran away from his people, told God he had the wrong guy to lead his people out of bondage, broke the first 10 commandments tablets in anger, etc. How about King David who sent his mistress', (Bathsheba) husband to his death to cover up his adulterous act—which resulted in her, becoming pregnant? Or how about the Apostle Paul (Saul) who routinely persecuted and murdered Christians?

GOD DOES NOT WANT YOU TO GIVE UP ON PURSUING A RELATIONSHIP WITH HIM.

Consider what Paul wrote in 1 Timothy 1:12-16 as evidence that if Paul, who was chosen by Christ to be his messenger to the Gentiles, can be forgiven for his sins—that you can be forgiven as well of your sins provided you repent with complete sincerity and make it a point to no longer pursue disobedience to God. Paul wrote, "How thankful I am to Christ Jesus our Lord for choosing me as one of his messengers, and giving me the strength to be faithful to him, **even though I used to** scoff at the name of Christ. I hunted down his people, harming them in every way I could. But God had mercy on me because I didn't know what I was doing, for I didn't know Christ at that time. Oh, how kind our Lord was, for he showed me how to trust him and become full of the love of Christ Jesus. How true it is, and how I long that everyone should know it, that Christ Jesus came into this world to save sinners—*and I was the greatest of them all.* But God had mercy on me so that Christ Jesus **could use me as an example to show everyone how patient he is with even the worst sinners** so that others will realize that they, too, can have everlasting life."

God wants to save you and He awaits the opportunity to do so patiently. He asks for so little in return really—but many find it difficult to give up the worldly ways that they are accustomed to. They want to chase money, power, sex, and all sorts of flashy new things. They are deceived that the next sexual partner, new drug, adding a few more digits to their bank account, a new leadership position, or the new sports car will make, and keep, them happy. It is all fleeting! We, humans, spend more time accumulating "stuff" that ultimately will be left for someone else to enjoy as we won't be able to take it with us upon death. Seems ridiculous when you really stop and think about it. But most of us continue to do just that.

Will we never learn? Satan is behind the spiritually bankrupt and broken system we find ourselves in. We think we need another new TV or boat, but never stop and think that maybe the money would be better served buying Bibles and handing them out. Or how about walking around handing out money to the poor? What about helping a fellow Christian start a small business? No, we couldn't do that! It's more important to us that we look good and important to our fellow man.

No matter whether you choose to truly know Christ is up to you. But the Bible makes it clear that sin cannot win and faith cannot fail! I simply ask what you really have to lose by believing, trusting, and obeying God. It is time you come out of your spiritual slumber and make it a point to fully know Jesus so that you may be saved and enjoy the promise of true happiness and everlasting life. God says your previous failures are indeed not final and He is waiting patiently to save you, but you must stretch out your hand to grasp His so that He can pull you away from your sin-filled life and adorn you in a new and better life.

CHAPTER 16

Changing Your Thought Life—Purification

Most people who begin a spiritual transformation by acknowledging Jesus suddenly realize they don't know what comes next. While they may accept the existence of God, and they have come to know about Christ and His wonderful sacrifice on the cross to buy back their lives, and they have repented of their sins and acknowledge Jesus as their Lord and Savior, they now ask themselves, "What do I do now?" "How will I keep free of sinning?"

The answers are you keep moving "forward" in your walk with Christ and you will never be able not to sin! Just because one becomes saved through belief and acknowledgment of Jesus as their Lord and Savior does not mean that their physical worldly life is now set to be easy. They will not be free of illness. They will not be guaranteed not to have money issues. They won't suddenly wake up and find that everyone likes them. No, none of these or any other multitude of everyday life issues will become non-existent in the life of a Christian. The one and only thing promised is everlasting eternal life with God. However, their new life will not begin until their current life is extinguished. Most of us are in no hurry to leave this world just so we can begin our new eternal lives. Nor should we be as human life is deemed to be precious by the Creator.

However, when we decide to now be committed to God, we are to change our approach to life. We are to now dismiss our "pride" and to walk with humility—just as the Lord did. We are to move from independence from God to dependence upon God! We acknowledge that our previous lives were incomplete, shallow, and self-centered. We want, and accept, that God is our master and we are His servant. We recognize that God created us for His pleasure—not the other way around. We understand that if God gives us a command it is for our benefit—not a control mechanism. In fact, Jesus will never make you do anything.

Thus, our thoughts and views begin to change for the better. We are accepting that we cannot, nor ever will we be able to, not sin. The only difference between a follower of Christ and a non-believer is the acceptance of Jesus as the Son of God who lived a sinless life in order to pay off the debt of man by sacrificing His blood upon the cross to wash away the sins of those who decide to believe and trust in Him. The believer also accepts that Jesus conquered death by rising from his tomb and is alive and in heaven once again. Both the believer and non-believer will both continue to sin—it's just that the follower of Jesus is stating that he knows he has been forgiven of his past sins and that he will now make a "conscious" decision to refrain from sinning in the future. If they should commit an unconscious sin, or commit a conscious sin but immediately confess it before God, then the believer knows that the sin is forgiven.

GOD MATURES US FOR AN INCREASINGLY-GREATER SPIRITUAL LOAD.

So you see, there is no special way to be eternally saved—just confession of one's sins to God with genuine repentance. No need to confess them before another man who really knows nothing about you or your motives. God knows when, why, how, where, and who may have been involved in the sin—your repentance is for your benefit, not God's. Confessing your sins to the Lord is part of the purification process in your life.

God seems to have designed his plan for mankind's salvation with an evolutionary process that leads us along a path of purification. For example, this is why even a Christian will continue to be tempted, and why they will encounter difficulties and challenges. In fact, sometimes some really bad things will occur even to the most steadfast believer. God is attempting to purify us for our future spiritual lives by making us battle-tested under fire. He showed us that He did not exempt even His Son to these temptations, sorrows, and challenges. Jesus saw friends die, He suffered tremendous pain, He had to go 40-days without food, Satan was allowed to tempt him, He was rejected by those He came to save, etc. So if God did not spare His own Son of these things, should we really expect for Him to do so for us? Obviously not.

We need to understand that God promises that we will never be expected to handle more than we can bear. Notice though that God is the one who decides what He knows we are able to withstand. He will, at times, *allow* us to be pushed right up to our breaking point. So why does he do this? In order to make us stronger!

God matures us for an increasingly-greater spiritual load. The only way to do this is to allow Satan and his followers to work against us. See the book of Job for further clarification of how the purification process works. God allowed Satan to do everything imaginable to Job—except to kill him. Satan was allowed to kill members of his family, take away his possessions, be shunned by friends, and even cover his skin in boils in an attempt to get Job to curse and turn his back on God. Satan failed! Job stayed true to God and was rewarded for his steadfastness to the Lord by receiving even more blessings than what he had previously had.

Are you prepared for such an onslaught from Satan? That is why God allows these difficulties to come into our lives. He wants to make sure we are ready for the next step planned in our spiritual evolution. This doesn't mean we have to "enjoy" the process—just be accepting and know that it is part of the process of purification of our spirit. Ultimately, God is looking for us to keep positively changing our thought life.

Before our spiritual transformation in following Christ, we usually did whatever our inclination led us to do. Now we realize the correct path is to do the opposite of what our human inclination tells us to do. For before we chose to sin—now we attempt to avoid sin. One thing the Lord hates more than just about anything else is "pride". We are warned over and over throughout the Bible to be cautious about our pride. Remember, it was pride that led to the fall of Lucifer from heaven. Therefore, God states on many occasions not to let ourselves be full of pride, but rather to follow the example of Jesus and to approach life with humility.

The Book of Proverbs is filled with verses about pride. Consider the following:

11:2 "Proud men end in shame, but the meek become wise."

13:10 "Pride leads to arguments; be humble, take advice and become wise."

16:3 "Pride disgusts the Lord. Take my word for it—proud men shall be punished."

16:18 "Pride goes before destruction and haughtiness before a fall."

18:12 "Pride ends in destruction; humility ends in honor."

I would think these should suffice in convincing you where God stands on the "pride" issue.

So, begin your new walk with humility and wisdom will follow you. Stay away from boasting about who you are and what you are capable of doing. Remember that is by the grace of God that you were given life and the DNA you possess to accomplish whatever "gifts" were given to you. You did nothing to earn these gifts! So please be humble. It is fine to have a "healthy" self-image—just do not become prideful.

Pride is nothing more than one's belief that they, or other humans, rather than God, is responsible for the outcome of their lives. Do not fall into this trap—it is the message of our adversary, the devil!

Start approaching each day with reverence and gratitude to your Creator. Be thankful for what you do have rather than envious of what you don't have. Recognize that somebody else out there has it as bad, or possibly even worse, than you do. We can all start feeling sorry for ourselves—but if we change our thought life as directed, we will begin to see that our world is more full than empty. Whenever I'm having a perceived tough time, I quickly remember my friend Les. He is one of the strongest spiritual warriors I know.

Les was involved in a very bad car accident in his youth. He was fortunate to survive the accident, but he suffered a significant injury to one of his legs—losing much of the musculature to the leg and severing his Sciatic nerve . The leg was so mutilated that the conveying wisdom was to amputate the leg. Fortunately for Les, a surgeon who was at the hospital that fateful evening had been a surgeon in Vietnam. He convinced others that the leg could be saved. The surgery was a success and despite needing a foot brace because of the Sciatic nerve damage, Les has been totally ambulatory and even played sports for recreation. He never let his "disability" hold him back from anything he wanted to achieve, and he has always had a great outlook on life. Unfortunately, this is not where Les' story of challenges and heartache ended. For over the next few years, Les lost first his mother, then his loving wife, and then his mother-in-law—all to breast cancer. He then lost his father-in-law to brain cancer—they were quite close. Then just a few months after burying his father-in-law, Les was faced with discovering his twenty-three-year old son, a college athlete, passed away with no apparent cause for his death. An autopsy was performed and yielded no closure as to the cause of death. Yet despite all this tragedy, Les never wavered in his belief that Christ loves him and had taken his loved ones for his reasons, which were unexplainable in human terms. I never once heard him question God, nor did he ever turn his back on his Savior. Les is a devout Catholic and attends worship services regularly.

So the next time you think you have it bad—think about my buddy Les—just as I do. Suddenly your world may be a little brighter than what you thought. However, my buddy Les, despite all his problems, may still not have had it as "bad" as the Apostle Paul. In 2 Corinthians 11:23-27, you can read how Paul outlines that he was shipwrecked three times, thrown in prison several times, whipped five times by the Jews, beaten on three separate occasions with metal rods, stoned once, under death threats innumerable times, had to sleep outside in the cold on many occasions with no shelter from the elements, and went without food for many days at a time—all because of his preaching of the gospel of Jesus.

The Apostle Paul sums up what my message in this section is all about. Turn to 2 Corinthians 7:10, "**For sometimes God uses sorrow in our lives to help us turn away from sin and seek eternal life. *We should never regret his sending it.* For the sorrow of the man who is not a Christian is not the sorrow of true repentance and does not prevent eternal death.**"

If you change your thought life and focus on the things that are indeed good, you can't possibly be thinking of evil at the same time. We are only able to have one thought in our minds at a single moment. If you choose to think of good and righteous thoughts, then you will be increasingly better equipped not to sin. Since it is impossible for a man to think two thoughts simultaneously, choose to pursue the thoughts that are measured as "good" by God, and you will be less apt to fall into sin, and not do the very things that lead you to disappointment.

Apostle Paul encourages us in Ephesians 6:10-13, "Finally, my brethren, be strong in the Lord and the power of His might. Put on the whole armor of God that you may be able to stand against the wiles of the devil. **For we do not wrestle against flesh and blood, but against principalities, against powers, against the *rulers* of the darkness of this age, against spiritual *hosts* of wickedness in high places. Therefore take up the whole armor of God, that you may be able to withstand the evil day, and having done all, to stand."**

CHAPTER 17

Why Me? Why Not Me?

It is our nature to always wonder in disbelief when something bad happens to us. We search for answers to help us make some sense as to why certain "things", particularly sorrowful ones, have been allowed to impact our lives. No one really can fully explain the mystery of why bad things happen to good folks. Tragedy and suffering have existed since the 'fall' in the Garden of Eden. God created a perfect world, and man, through the influence of Satan, messed it up. God did create a world with a *potential* for evil to exist, but it was a man who brought forth the evil by following Satan instead of God.

Here are a few essential pieces of information:

1. God the Father did not spare his own Son from sorrow. Jesus was close to Lazarus and it pained Him that His friend died before He arrived.

2. God the Father required His own Son experience horrible physical pain. The beatings and the crucifixion were unbearable.

3. God the Father requires His Son to experience betrayal, slander, rejection, and many other negative human emotions.

So ask yourself, if He allowed this to be done to His Son, what expectation should we have that we would not have to suffer similar things in our life as Christians?

Romans 8:28 says, "And we know that all things work together for good to those who love God, to those who are called **according to His purpose.**"

Again we see that God has a purpose in all things. You see God either *directs* (Great flood, Passover, etc.) *or permits* things to happen to us. He is God so He is fully aware of what you will experience. This does not mean that He takes any pleasure to watch one's suffering—the opposite is true. However, if you love God, you understand that He has a plan for you, and it may be nothing like you have chosen for yourself. **His ways are not our ways.** However, what is being done must be looked upon as having a reason that you cannot fully understand at this time. You may count on it being revealed to you at the appointed time—not before. This is very difficult for us humans to grasp, but the more readily we accept His decision, the better off we will be going forward.

Sometimes we pray for things that God deems as not being in our best interests; of course, we have no idea that what we are asking is not appropriate for us. We grumble and sometimes even plead our case with God. Still, He won't relent to our desires. But God always does things for His glory and for our benefit. He may not let us keep a loved one, may not let us have a certain job, win the lottery, etc., but rest assured it is out of love for us that the decision is made. Acceptance that His decisions are right should be enough for any believer.

Take for example that God has refused to allow you to get the promotion for a position that opened recently. You prayed and asked daily to get that promotion—but then another person gets that position. You become distraught and wonder why doesn't God love you enough to give you a chance. However, two months after, the man that took the position is let go because the corporation has decided the job is no longer necessary. Now how do you feel about His decision?

GOD DIRECTS OR PERMITS THINGS TO HAPPEN TO US. HE WORKS IN MYSTERIOUS WAYS.

Likewise, some are allowed greater riches in this life than others. Again, it is permitted or directed by God. We can sit around and try to explain why some seemingly less than stellar folks are blessed with full bank accounts, nice homes, cars, health—while others struggle to make ends meet. Again, you must trust God to choose to allow things to happen for a reason of His choosing. Maybe some of us will have greatness in heaven that we did not experience on earth. His plan is His plan.

Deaths of loved ones are probably the hardest to make any sense out of spiritually. We feel "robbed or cheated" when someone for whom we care deeply is no longer in our life. Sometimes it borders on unbearable. There are no words of real comfort, and every explanation offered up by our fellow humans is shallow at best. I have no explanation for death—other than a biblical one. Death was never supposed to exist. It was brought on by the sin of man—including our own sins. I wish it did not exist but there is no escaping physical death. However, we are to know that death will have no power over us in the next life.

You need to comprehend that this physical life you currently have is not really what you were designed to be. We simply have a body that is nothing more than a container to hold our soul. This life we live here with all its pitfalls and suffering is only meant to test us and prepare us for what is to come. Our life after this will no longer be one of pain, death, and sorrow. Our new lives will be filled with happiness, power, and honor, and our spiritual bodies will be immortal—the exact opposite as is the case currently, which is the result of sin. You see outwardly we are dying, but inwardly our eternal soul continues to grow and evolve. God is able to look inside of us, at our souls and examine our hearts (mind) and determine whether we are reaching a point of spirituality He has chosen.

Thus, God may use suffering and tragedy to draw us or someone else closer to Him. He may use it to mold us and/or others into the shape He destines for our future. Ultimately it is our decision whether or not we accept His decisions and His promises that a time is approaching whereby there will be no more pain and suffering, no tears and we will be reunited with God.

Here is our Lord's promise from Revelation 21:4, "He will wipe away every tear from their eyes, and death shall be no more, neither shall there be mourning, nor crying, nor pain anymore, for the former things have passed away." Your new life will be one without the boundaries of time, gravity, dimensional movement, nutrition (although we will eat and drink if we wish), etc. Great joy will occupy your soul at all times.

In our present state of existence, we realize that stress and problems are inevitable due to sin having entered the world. We understand that no amount of preparation can adequately ready us for many of the problems we will face in our lives—things like the loss of a loved one or the loss of a job. We should be comforted by these words uttered by our Lord Jesus in John 16:33, "I have said these things to you, that in me you may have peace. **In the world you will have tribulation. But take heart; I have overcome the world.**" We know from this that Jesus is emphatically stating that He has already conquered this world and every type of trouble that may come our way. Jesus is not denying that trouble will come knocking on your door. He makes no promise of smooth sailing for the Christian, but He gives us the Word of God as our refuge in our times of need.

I am very reluctant to share this personal story with you as I do not wish to make any of this message about me—but I feel compelled to do so. I ask that you have no pity for me, but will gladly accept prayers of healing and strength.

A while ago within a span of three months, I was diagnosed with a chronic disease, one of my sister's died, death took my best friend of thirty-nine years, and my wife's cousin died. I felt pretty low, to say the least. However, I went through all five stages of grief (denial, anger, bargaining, depression, and acceptance) just like everyone else. During the first four stages, I continued to spar with God over writing this book. I was obstinate and I bargained that if He would just heal me then I would do whatever He asked. Of course, I knew better—I didn't say I'm always the smartest person. Finally, I came to my senses and accepted my diagnosis, and accepted that God's plans for those I loved no longer were a concern of mine. I came to understand that He wanted me to write this book of explanation as there was no telling when my human time may come to an end—meaning it could be today or twenty years from now, but the time for writing was right now! I pray that my children, my wife, all my relatives, my friends and YOU will be smarter than me and follow the path laid before you by God. Use those "gifts" and talents provided to you for His glory without delay as you will be better for it in all ways and a sense of peace will come upon you, unlike anything you have ever experienced.

I attended a healthcare conference once where the speaker was making the analogy that our lives are like one of those long narrow candles. At the time of our birth, the candle is lit and provides "light" to others with whom we interact. Some of us certainly burn brighter and/or have longer lives than others. The key the speaker said was indeed to burn brighter than others in the room, or any other situation, so as to give others feelings of goodness, to model for them a life filled with integrity, hope, and determination. He then stated that another key was to do this from the earliest point in your life as possible so that you would have more time to have a positive impact on others. He noted that your candle (life) could be extinguished at any time even though your candle looked much longer than others surrounding you. The speaker said that everyone in the room should leave that day realizing that they may have already lost many years of valuable time to be beneficial to others. When I look back now, with at least 2/3rds of my life in the rearview mirror, and having denied God's "calling" for me to use my "gift", I am ashamed. Please be better than me, and realize your candle may be burning at a very fast rate that you are unable to recognize. Be the light that God wants you to be, and burn as bright as you can for His glory, for as long as you can! In this way, you will help others through times of suffering, tragedy—and even in good and joyful times.

Only Jesus who overcame and conquered this world can give us the peace we are seeking in times of tragedy and suffering. Look to Christ for your comfort whenever you are in need of help, guidance, and strength to help you through the crises that you undoubtedly have to face.

CHAPTER 18

Satan's Tools

Guilt, Worry, Doubt, Discouragement, and More

We are frequently reminded in the Holy Scriptures to not fall prey to guilt and/or worry. The vast majority of humans spend an inordinate amount of time dwelling upon the past or focusing on the future. This is not to say thinking about the past so as not to repeat sins or mistakes does not have any value. Nor is it not of value to take some time to consider our future.

However, when we become preoccupied with thoughts about our past undoubtedly guilt rears its ugly head. And when we become preoccupied with thoughts about our future—well that is when worry creeps into the picture. We should not as believers of Christ spend our time endlessly rehashing the past or thinking about our future.

As Christians, we need to remember that once we have repented and confessed of our sins they are not to be brought forth again. When we do this, out of guilt, we are denying that God has already, as He has stated, forgiven us of those horrendous sins. In a sense, we are saying we don't trust that Jesus did die to forgive us of those sins. I doubt any of us sets out with the intent of stating that God does not fulfill promises. If we continue to ask for forgiveness for the same sins over and over and question how it is possible that God could love me—then we are not controlling our thought life and we have opened our minds once again to Satan. Recall that Satan will constantly attempt to convince you that whatever you have done or will do will not be forgiven. Do not let him in! Rebuke him in the name of Jesus, and tell him that you will not argue with him, but that you are absolutely certain, as promised, that your sins have been forgiven. Satan is a master debater and you can't win—so simply lean on the Word of God and remind him that you are not inviting him inside. If you do this, Satan will realize his guilt trip no longer works on you and he will move on to easier prey.

Likewise, Satan will also manipulate you into worrying about your future. The same approach - rebuke him in Jesus' name and tell him to move along. Worry is about things beyond our control anyway. We don't even know if we will awaken tomorrow, let alone 10 years from now. Again this is not to say that a little thought to the future—like having a retirement plan is a bad thing. It isn't bad at all! It only becomes problematic when we decide to fixate on what we are doing tomorrow, next week, 10 years from now, etc. When this happens, life passes us by and we may finally awaken from our worry slumber and realize that we feel like crap, our children are grown, our spouse moved out, and the dog died. But isn't it great we have a bunch of money on paper sitting in an account at some bank that now we are too sick to spend, our kids don't like us, we are going to give away half to our "ex" and their new spouse, and the last thing we are considering is getting another dog— all because we chose to fixate about "tomorrow."

THE REASON WE DON'T RECOGNIZE SATAN IS BECAUSE HIS VOICE IS IDENTICAL TO OUR OWN.

Do not let Satan destroy your life by causing you to worry so much about the future that life seemingly moved at warp speed.

Instead, live life with hope in the here and now. It is called the present—and indeed it is a "present" from God! Each and every breath we take, every heartbeat we have, every smile we give or receive, are true blessings from God. We all do not spend enough time in thanks to the Lord for our lives. Will any of us go to our deaths thinking about our bank account balances?

No, we will be thinking of our loved ones, like the birth of our children, the day we met our spouse, a special vacation or something similar to these. We will not be thinking about the day we beat our business associate in some deal or the time we bought our last car.

So let us look at what Jesus said in Matthew 6:25-27, "So my counsel is: Don't worry about things—food, drink, and clothes. For you already have life and a body—and they are far more important than what to eat or wear. Look at the birds! They do not worry about what to eat—they don't need to sow or reap or store up food—for your heavenly Father feeds them. And you are far more valuable to him than they are. *Will all your worries add a single moment to your life?*"

Also, did you know that Jesus never possessed a home? That he never had a bed to call his own—instead he slept outdoors most nights. When his disciples were worried about a storm on the Sea of Galilee they woke Him up from His sleep to ask for help and they were surprised He didn't even show concern for the storm. Jesus modeled what we should do; He never worried about anything!

Of course, as God, Jesus didn't need to worry—but He was setting an example in His human form that worry and guilt should have no power over one that is full of faith. We should always have trust in God as he is always faithful. He keeps his promises!

Worry is something we all struggle with because it is akin to a constant, uninvited, unwanted companion. I know from personal experience that worry is like a giant leech that grabs hold of you and won't let go until it sucks all the life from you. But we must break its grip for Jesus is essentially telling us that it is sinful to worry because it is an overzealous concern of future events for which we cannot control. Philippians 4:16 says. "Do not be **anxious** about anything." And Luke 12:29, "Therefore I say to you, **do not worry** about your life, what you will eat; nor about the body, what you will put on."

We humans worry and feel guilty because of our inborn propensity to want to be accepted. Instead, we are full of feelings of rejection which goes back again to the Garden of Eden when God rejected humanity dwelling in paradise, because of the sin they exhibited. We have been attempting ever since that time to fill the void of rejection with wanting to be considered acceptable. Again, we failed to understand that the acceptance we needed was from God for we decided that we would take acceptance from mankind. This is a poor substitute and will never be spiritually fulfilling. Look at how advertisers, for example, play upon this need to be accepted. They tell us what we should want to wear, drive, eat, look like, use, buy, etc. We then do as they say because we want to fit in and be accepted by the cool people. When will we learn that nothing will ever fulfill the void left by God's rejection of us—except God returning to fill that void.

Satan uses many tools to attempt to control the minds of humans. Besides guilt and worry, he uses doubt, anger, pride, envy, jealousy, greed, and a vast amount of other tools at his disposal. However, it would appear that his favorite tool to use on us is discouragement. Discouragement has several synonyms—disheartedness, dispiritedness, dejection, depression, demoralization, disappointment, despondency, hopelessness, gloom, despair, and pessimism.

Thus, do not let your mind become discouraged. I know it is easy to say and hard to do—but God is always with us, even when it appears He is not there or even listening. He will never abandon you even in the most troubled times. Again, at the time you are being allowed to be manipulated by Satan—just stay strong and know that the Lord will never reject or disavow a believer. He loves his own too much to ever forsake them. While your walk with God is never going to be a casual stroll through life; it remains important to never give up on His power to rescue us from even the worst case scenarios imaginable. Resist discouragement and stay enthused about Christ and inevitably you will lead a purposeful life.

CHAPTER 19

Eternal Life

This is the goal of every Christian. We desire to be with the Lord free of the container of our fleshly bodies. We Christians know from the Word of God that a better place awaits us than this physical world. We strive to purify ourselves daily in ways that will better prepare us for our lives beyond the grave.

Here is Jesus' promise in John 3:18, "**There is no eternal doom awaiting those who *trust* him (Jesus) to save them. But those who don't trust him have already been tried and condemned for not believing in the only Son of God.**"

Note that Jesus made this statement while in conversation with the Jewish religious leaders (Pharisees) during his time on earth. This was said to show condemnation of them—but it was also left for future generations to come to their senses and acknowledge who He is and what He has done for them via the cross. Thus, you and every other person born since Jesus made this bold statement has a decision to make in order to assure that their souls will have eternal life. Failure to understand that his blood was poured out to repay the sins of all mankind is spiritual suicide. Don't make the mistake of not recognizing Him for who He is and what He has done for you.

God even loves the sinner—but how much more He loves those who believe in His Son and are willing to confess their sins to Him and repent of their wickedness. Jesus was asked why He consorted with known sinners, even going to their homes to eat. He told the religious leaders that He had not come to save the saved—but to save the unsaved. Jesus showed compassion and kindness to all. He wants all of mankind to be saved. He gave all of us the gift of the comforter (Holy Spirit) when he departed mankind physically. He told us to lean on the Holy Spirit for strength in all matters.

Please realize that the Holy Spirit of God dwells in every person that is a believer in Jesus Christ. While some may contend that the Holy Spirit is within the believer and also the non-believer—there is not one verse in Scripture that states this as fact. So any attempt to convince one that a non-believer has the Holy Spirit within them should not be accepted. Only some "commentary" has been used to attempt to prove this point.

Here is an analogy to help one understand that the Holy Spirit is ever ready to move into a new believer at the moment they accept and state that Jesus is their Master, Savior, and High

Priest. The Holy Spirit is like an expert home remodeler who can't wait until you call them and ask them to come in and totally renovate your dwelling. The Holy Spirit is there patiently waiting for your call to accept Christ and be invited to come into your essence—his hand is literally at the doorknob. The moment that you, with full sincerity, admit that you are a sinner and you accept that Jesus died and shed his blood in order to save you from destruction—the Holy Spirit takes that as an invitation to enter your body and to immediately begin leading you on a path to totally remodel your life.

ACCEPT THE FREE GIFT
OF GOD'S GRACE!

When one moves from non-belief to faith in Christ, the Holy Spirit begins to ignite a fire within us. Prior to receiving the Holy Spirit, our spiritual homes (body) are like a home with an inactive furnace. The moment we acknowledge Jesus as our personal Lord and Savior, the furnace suddenly receives a pilot light. As our faith is professed a little more, we see the pilot light kicks on a small burner and the Holy Spirit begins to burn a little more intensely within. With each passing day of faith, and even from moment to moment, we begin to feel differently. We then begin to act differently and speak differently—better, more helpful, less judgmental, kinder, more compassionate, etc. We begin to understand that all God wants is our obedience to His commands. And as we obey God the Holy Spirit fills us up more and more and we become like a roaring spiritual bonfire. We are full of joy that we never experienced prior to our conversion to our grace filled faith.

One's goal for their soul should be easy to see, but for some, it remains hidden. Our life is not meant to be completed upon this planet, rather we are to aspire to greatness beyond these fleshly bodies that we currently inhabit. When we accept the free gift of God's grace and He sends His Holy Spirit to fill the void in our souls, we begin to "know" that earth is not the final destination. Instead, we recognize that we want to be where our Lord dwells continually—Heaven.

Consider the following from Romans 3:21-24, "But now the righteousness of God apart from the law is revealed, being witnessed by the Law and the Prophets, even the righteousness of God, through faith in Jesus Christ, to all and on all who believe. For there is no difference; **for all have sinned and fall short of the glory of God**, being justified freely by His grace through the redemption that is Christ Jesus,"

If you wish to get to Heaven and have eternal life and bask in the glory of the Creator, then it becomes evident that you will not be able to do so by "being good enough" or keeping the Laws handed to Moses. Instead, you will need to be acquitted of your sin by God and the only way that can happen is if you willingly and wholeheartedly accept and trust (grace) that only through Jesus Christ can your sins be taken away.

Only through this gift of grace will you, or any other human, be found to be acceptable to God. We see that God used the blood of his Son to wash away the stain of our sins in order to save us from His wrath of judgment.

CHAPTER 20

Price of Disobedience

Many people fail to understand that discipline in our lives is a good thing. To God, we are His children and he knows that failure to discipline us (disobedience) would be akin to spiritual abuse. That is why, at times, we encounter difficulties. Whenever we stray too far from Him—He allows something to happen to us that gets our attention and makes us look to Him for guidance/help. His ways are always right and are done to help spare us further issues.

As a parent would you let your young children *choose* their own way of doing things? Of course not! They might choose to cook marshmallows over an open fire in your living room. Instead, you teach them how to choose the most appropriate way to accomplish something. It is the same with God since the "fall." God has been attempting to show us the way to salvation ever since we disobeyed in Eden. He does this to bring us back into the relationship that was intended from the beginning of mankind. He knew then, and now, that the path we chose was one that set us up for spiritual failure. Disobedience to God is iniquity—the very same thing Lucifer did in heaven.

We live in an ever-increasing culture, that is clearly ruled by the "Prince of this world." In John 14:29-30, Jesus is describing his passion, death, and resurrection to his disciples and concludes by saying, "I have told you this before it happens, so that when it happens, you may believe. I will no longer speak much with you, for the ruler of this world is coming. **He has no power over me.**"

And thus, Jesus does use the phrase "ruler of this world," (or "Prince of this world" in many translations) thereby indicating that *Satan has some power and influence here.* However, whatever influences that Satan possesses—it is clear that Jesus has ultimate power as He is the true King of the universe, and thereby sets limits on Satan's power and can overrule Satan at any point.

Jesus explains later that the prince of this world now stands condemned as a result of His (Jesus) conquering death upon the cross and rising to once again take His seat upon His throne—see John 12:31 and John 16:11.

The title "Prince of this world" is ultimately only written upon the hearts of those who have refused the absolute authority of God and accepted the practical authority of the devil. Sadly, through these misguided souls, Satan exerts his influence and power upon the earth. However, the Christian understands that while Satan's evil activity at times seems intense, **it always remains secondary to God's power** who permits this immoral and disgusting influence only so that a greater good will come from it.

Satan's influence is to create disobedience in man as it relates to God's commands. By the look of the state of the world today Satan's business (disobedience) is quite profitable! The evil one wants us to simply do ONE of the following:

1. Deny that God exists.
2. Deny that Jesus is your Lord and Savior.
3. Worship Satan—or worship the world.

The adversary is diligent in his approach and always ready to enter one's mind if given even a small opportunity. He knows if he can create the slightest doubt to the sovereignty of God he will triumph over you. Or if he can call into question the deity of Jesus Christ in your thoughts—he has you. If he can convince you that life is really just whatever you want it to be (worldly worship) he has made another convert.

1 Peter 5:8 states, "Be sober, be vigilant; because your adversary the devil walks about like a roaring lion, seeking whom he may devour." Therefore, you need to be constantly on the lookout for the evil one who remember can even disguise himself as someone you are led to believe is totally trustworthy. You must be prepared to sum a person up rather quickly and to be always aware of your surroundings. You need to be able to discern what is being said to you—so that you are not overwhelmed quickly even by one you thought you knew well.

It is my belief that we are to seek to attain Maximum Spiritual Maturity (MSM). As we see from the scripture above, Satan is like a lion constantly looking for someone to devour. He especially has a taste for Christians.

How do lions hunt? If you recall, it is the female lions of the pride that do most of the hunting. Lions hunt animals, like gazelles, wildebeests or antelope as preferred prey. In a coordinated attack lions attempt to single out one animal in the herd that has wandered off due to injury, age, or lack of focus. Once they have that animal surrounded the attack is mounted with frequent success.

Satan, our adversary, hunts just like a lion. The most vulnerable prey for him to devour are "immature" Christians, or those that have lost their way because they have failed to be on their guard. Many animal species recognize that there is a certain safety in numbers. This is why we see schools of fish, flocks of sheep, herds of cattle, gaggles of geese, etc. However, it is to my surprise that many Christians attempt to go it alone, or worse are brought into the faith and then left by fellow Christians to flounder on their own.

We see churches all over that make disciple-making a priority, but are lacking when it comes to helping the immature Christian in his or her walk. Many Christians need to make protecting new Christians, as well as those who need additional guidance in God's word, a matter of greatest importance.

In order to assist Christians in achieving MSM, we need to make sure they understand the importance of regular and frequent reading of God's word. We need to teach them the importance of fellowship and surrounding ourselves with other people who are strong in their faith. We need to encourage and demonstrate that going to church is important because of its ability to show us the power of hearing the word of God from the mouths of others. All of these things are examples that will help to mentor these immature and/or struggling faith seekers so as not to lose them to the lion who seeks to devour them.

DISOBEDIENCE TO GOD IS INIQUITY — THE SAME THING LUCIFER DID IN HEAVEN.

When we are vulnerable and most apt to disobey God is when we are not focused and immersed in His word. Thus, it is vital that you know God's commands and that if a person should attempt to steer you toward disobedience to God, then you should immediately rebuke them. Note what Jesus said to his disciple Peter in Mark 8:33, "But when Jesus turned and looked at his disciples, he rebuked Peter." Get behind me, Satan!" he said. *"You do not have in mind the concerns of God, but merely human concerns."*

Jesus did this to Peter as a result of Peter asking him to "tone" down his speech regarding his impending death and resurrection. In doing so, Jesus is making the case that any man, even His own disciple, could lapse in spirit momentarily and allow Satan to do what he does—lie, distort, question God, etc. This should distinctly show how cautious we must be to make sure that we gauge and filter things going on around us. However, one needs to understand that just as each of us has a different threshold for pain—likewise it is with a person's ability to hear or watch certain things. For example, you may not be able to help a bleeding and mangled person. Thank goodness that doctors, nurses and EMTs can. Thus, it is important to note what may bother one person has little effect on another because of certain traits bestowed upon them. However, one is not to break God's commands in order to justify something they may do—which would be like someone saying that they should watch pornography for some contorted reason. That will never fly in God's eyes!

If a person believes something is inherently wrong, then it is a sin. If on the other hand, a person does not even "think" upon what they are doing then it can't be sin unless the thought(s) are in contrast to those items that God has already clearly stated are sins. Meaning even if you didn't believe that murder was wrong because no one ever told you that murdering someone is "wrong", you can't simply think it must be okay to murder someone, and that God will forgive you of the murder you commit. This is because you are supposed to understand from the age of discernment that life is precious and that you can't just go around killing folks.

So at the very heart of unrighteousness is disobedience to the commandments of God. Look at Romans 5:19, "Adam caused many to be sinners because he **disobeyed** God, and Christ caused many to be made acceptable to God because he **obeyed**." Jesus modeled what a righteous life should look like, and we in turn as followers of Christ choose to obey God.

Thus, to be righteous in God's eyes we willingly choose to obey His commands. Lucifer obviously chose to disobey—then other angels followed Lucifer—Eve did—and Adam did as well. It was this sin of disobedience that led to separation from God, damage to our DNA, and the entrance of death to our existence.

Our failure in the Garden of Eden to recognize that the request for obedience was not done as a punishment to man but rather placed upon us to provide us with the discipline to protect us from things beyond our mortal senses. Unfortunately, we failed to see that God loved us so much that He created the plan of obedience for our own benefit.

The only reason that one refuses to accept God (obey) as the center of their life is because of their unwillingness to give up control of their life. This is a huge mistake and makes us, in appearance to God, as we would see a vicious or rabid dog. The vicious dog is also unwilling to yield to his handler/master and obey the commands given to him. The Lord Jesus Christ is our Master and many of us refuse to yield to him. Are we not any better than the dog in this illustration?

Satan has many "tools" at his disposal so be constantly on the lookout for his tricks to influence you to disobey God.

CHAPTER 21

Our War with God—Futile

We, humans, are at war with God. Does this statement surprise you?

You see, we have enmity toward God. That is to say, we harbor hostility, animosity, ill-will and/or a strong dislike for God. Look at Romans 8:7, "Because the old sinful nature within us is against God. It never did obey God's laws and it never will." This verse clearly states that man chose to follow the desires of the fleshly mind rather than the desires of the spiritual mind. The result is that man clearly chose disobedience over obedience to God.

In turn, God looked upon this as a war against him—rebellion. He then began to pull away from us by no longer choosing to spend as much time walking and talking to Adam and Eve. However, while He withheld a full relationship with us by no longer doing as much with us, He did not abandon us and already had a plan ready to set in motion to bring us back into an originally designated relationship. God loves us so much that he did not destroy us, for He had reason to, for our disobedience.

Due to our fall from the grace of God in the garden, we clearly indicated to God that we preferred to follow the desires of our flesh more than the desires of our spirit. And for the most part, mankind will continue to do so right up until the moment of Jesus' second coming.

OUR REBELLION AGAINST GOD IS UNACCEPTABLE TO HIM.

However, we true Christians are to be constantly striving toward ending this rebellion toward God by placing our faith in the Lord Jesus. It was Jesus who told us that we were to love even our enemies. In Matthew 5:43-48 Jesus instructs us that we are to be like the Father who sees to it that the righteous and unrighteous alike get to bask in the sunlight of the Creator or have the rain fall upon them all. We are to strive to be perfect just as the Heavenly Father is perfect.

Even Christians struggle daily with accepting the Word of God because His Word goes against our sinful nature. This is why we are at enmity with God, for we have such a difficult time accepting that His Word is TRUE and always leads to a better life for us. We believe, as a result of our sinfulness, that we alone are masters over our lives. We think God is not really needed in our lives on a regular basis—so God doesn't call us, and believe that we will call Him if we need something. If we decide not to always put God first in our lives, and make conscious decisions not to obey His commands, then we set ourselves up for all sorts of problems. Christians are supposed to know better—but many are casual Christians who outside of church rarely seek to read the Word of God—thereby failing God's number one commandment. We are to follow Deuteronomy 6:5 which says, "You shall love the Lord your God with all your heart, with all your soul, and with all your strength." The way to Love (respect) God is to immerse yourself in His Word—this is to obey Him!

We are witnesses to a battle over our mind between our Lord and Satan. God solely communicates with us through the mind (heart)—Satan uses greed like wealth attainment, jealousy/envy by making you an adulterer or fornicator by using sex as a weapon, or intelligence/education so you feel smarter than others—who simply follow the "mythology" of God. You can clearly see both want to claim us as theirs. The biggest difference is that God wants to have a complete relationship with us. He allows us to say no to His ways and His requests, and He takes no pleasure in seeing us lead a life that ends in eternal bondage. God wants us to choose to follow Him as it for our own good and it gives Him glory. It hurts him deeply when we refuse to create a full relationship with Him, but He will not force Himself upon us. He leaves "us alone" if that is what we desire—but at the same time is ready to rescue us if we will simply acknowledge Him and repent.

Satan, on the other hand, is that same old cunning creature from the Garden of Eden who wants nothing more than the destruction of humanity—which is by alienating human beings from God. He will do this by any means available to him, but ultimately he is out to conquer you through the mind. Satan wants to control your thought life by corrupting your thoughts as to what is good and what is evil. In this way, he conquers you and pulls you away from Jesus. When Satan is able to finally control your thoughts and attitudes it becomes very difficult to escape his grasp. He makes us become conditioned to the stimulus he provides regularly that makes us do things contrary to God.

I, just like you, have sinned. I am ashamed to admit most of my life I have unconsciously followed Satan by believing in the accumulation of things, free love, and by creating my own legend of myself. What a pathetic creature I have been! However, I have been doing my best to turn my life toward God only. It is all that anyone can ask of you as well.

CHAPTER 22

God's Love

Jesus loves every one of us as if we are His children. As the father of three daughters, I know that my love for each of them has no boundary. I love them despite the fact that over their short lives they have disrespected me, cursed at me, told me they "hated" me, disobeyed me, taken things from me, dishonored me as well as some other things. However, I love them more today than the first time I saw them. I cannot fathom the thought of losing one of them, or one of them choosing to never see or talk to me again. I continually forgive them of everything they do or have done to me—for I love them despite all their faults.

This is how it is with God. He wants to be in your life. He loves you despite all the things you have done in disobedience to Him, dishonoring Him, cursing Him, hating Him, disrespecting Him, telling Him you didn't need Him, worshipping idols (money, cars, clothes, famous folks, etc.); yet He stands patiently ready to forgive you right now if you will simply express your love for Him through accepting that His Son died for all of your sins.

GOD IS ALWAYS READY TO WELCOME YOU WITH OPEN ARMS.

He is always right next to you awaiting your invitation to invite Him into your life. The second you tell Him of your desire for Jesus to come into your heart and that you accept Him for who is he is, then the Holy Spirit rushes in to start rebuilding the neglected temple within you.

Please call upon the Lord so that you might have the peace you have been searching for all of your life. Accept with open arms the grace (unmerited love of God) that will be provided to you by repenting of your sins and surrendering yourself through the acknowledgment of Jesus Christ as your personal Lord and Savior. Yes, it's that easy!

CHAPTER 23

Grace Costs You Nothing— But It Is Priceless

You can't purchase the grace of God with good works or money. So put away your thoughts that if you can just do a little more for God, He will smile down upon you and give you the grace (peace) you are seeking.

"I AM!"

It should be apparent to you that the cost of grace is far beyond all the world's assets combined! No amount of any combination of precious metals and stones could ever equal the priceless sacrifice of Jesus. It cost Him His earthly life by the exsanguination of His body's blood. His blood was the only acceptable payment for mankind's penalty of sin. In addition, it permanently, now and forever, broke the power of sin to rule the lives of those who follow Christ. And, disciples of Christ are promised **everlasting life whereby sin no longer exists.**

So I ask you, is one not better off to "believe" in Jesus, or risk their eternity? Surrender and follow God and you will feel the "chains" limiting your true potential fall to the ground in defeat.

CHAPTER 24

The True Path

In John 14:6-7 Jesus Christ makes one of the most important statements in the Holy Scriptures while speaking to his disciple, Thomas. Here is what Jesus said to Thomas in response to him asking if he would just show him the Father, then he would happy.

"I am the way—yes and the truth and the life. No one can get to the Father except through me. If you *had* known who I am, then you would have known who my Father is. From now on you know him—*and have seen him!*"

In distinguishing Himself as THE WAY, Jesus is clearly indicating that only through Him can a person achieve true salvation. He is stating that only He is the one true path or route to the Father and therefore to Heaven. Any other path is false and will lead to destruction. Only He can be the conduit, as He came here for the purpose of re-establishing a real relationship with God the Father.

This direct connection which had been severed, except through the occasional prophet sent by God, was now being opened up once again through Jesus. Jesus would now serve as man's High Priest in heaven and that all prayer and supplication were now to go through Him in His name. Only then would it be shared with the Father.

More importantly, Jesus is making a very bold claim in the times in which He lived as a human. He is stating that He is indeed God. Of course, as previously presented, Jesus made several affirmations that He was God. Some can't seem to comprehend this and attempt to explain away that Jesus doesn't really come out and utter that he is God. Those that do this forget the times in which these statements were disclosed, and that God had indicated that He would for His purposes make some things more difficult to understand than other things. This is not to say that God's Word is not clear—it is! However, as "fallen" beings, we have sin within us that can cloud our understanding and leads us to distortions that others we may have listened to or read have presented. It is best that a person look at as much evidence as possible from various sources instead of following one doctrine. Thus, the consensus of the many in almost all walks of life tends to be the most appropriate.

An example of this could be like asking one hundred (100) people for the best (fastest) way from point A to point B. Ninety-eight (98) people might say the best way to get from A to B is to take such and such a way. But two (2) people may say to take this other convoluted route, which just so happens is the only way they know how to get there. So which one will you take? I hope you said the one that the majority thought was best.

Interpretation of Scripture is done in the same way. Following one or two denominations interpretation may be misguided as many students and scholars over the past 3,400-1,900 (depending upon what book is being examined) years have come to a consensus that this scripture is saying ABC.

When we attempt to understand the Word of God, we must pray and ask that God help remove our strongly held biases and presuppositions. This can be very difficult particularly as we age. It becomes increasingly more and more difficult over time for us to let go and open our mind to what the Holy Spirit may be trying to tell us. I know at times it has been for me personally, so I would, therefore imagine this to be true for most. Humility and one's willingness to admit the possibility of having been mistaken are sometimes hard to do.

So, it is my humble opinion, and that of the vast majority of Christians, that Jesus is saying that He is God and that He, for His own purposes, chose a particular time in human history to take on the appearance of a man—Jesus. He did so to teach

"The Way" back to salvation. Jesus modeled the type of "life" that God the Father had intended mankind to follow—and He did this by always choosing to disclose "the truth".

Mark 2:5-7 clearly shows what blasphemy was considered during the time of Jesus. It reads, "**When Jesus saw how strongly they believed he would help, Jesus said to the sick man, "Son, *your sins are forgiven*!**" But some of the **Jewish religious leaders said to themselves as they sat there, "What? This is blasphemy! *Does he think he is God?* For only God can forgive sins!"**

At this moment in time, it is clear to the Jewish leaders that Jesus is without question placing Himself in the position of God the Father. Any other interpretation of this scripture would not be consistent with the backdrop presented.

Jesus doubles down on this claim when He is facing the Jewish religious leaders of the Sanhedrin after his arrest. In Matthew 27:63 the Jewish High Priest says, " **I demand in the name of the Living God that you tell us whether or not you claim to be the Messiah, the Son of God.**" "**Yes, Jesus said, I am.**" There is more scripture that follows, but I have stopped here for you to be able to concentrate on this statement.

Jesus is stating not only is He the Son of God, but that He is God! Look closely at His response—it does not read "Yes, I am—Jesus said. The way it is said with separation and emphasis on the "I am" is His way of pointing directly at his deity as the Living God. As a result of this statement, the Jewish High Priest tears his robe and makes it clear that Jesus is claiming to be equal with God. Note that in Jewish religious tradition nothing was ever construed to suggest that the arrival of the Messiah (deliverer) was to be a Divine being or to be equal in power to that of God. In His answer, Jesus is making it clear to the High Priest that He is indeed equal to God. And by His saying He would come again riding the clouds, He was emphatic that He was God and would be worshipped—which was reserved only for God.

As stated, there are many scriptures supporting the claim of Christ as God, but I would ask you to read John 8:58-59. "Very truly I tell you, Jesus answered, before Abraham was born, I am! At this, they picked up stones to stone him, but Jesus hid himself, slipping away from the temple grounds." You see, they were ready to stone Jesus because Jesus was stating that He was the great I AM (God) that had revealed Himself to Moses.

The bottom line here is that Jesus has stated that He is the only way (path) a person needs, the only truth (His words) one needs to know and the only real life (salvation) that exists. No one else can make this claim, and if they do they are to be considered a false god.

If you are continually looking for a particular scripture verse whereby Jesus says, "Hey, look I am God!" you will not find one. However, if you fail to see that Jesus does indeed, on several occasions, state in clear concise language for *first century Jews* to understand that He is saying He is God, then your eyes are being veiled. One may be able to explain away the words that Jesus chooses to use, BUT you can't dismiss the reaction to His words (**His meaning**) by those living at the time. To them, Jesus has said, "Hey, look I am God!"

THE ONLY PATH TO OUR HEAVENLY FATHER IS THROUGH JESUS.

You should by now seeing Christ for who e truly is. The Creator, the Ancient of Days, Yahweh, Jehovah, Lord Almighty. Jesus wants us to know who He is—He is not some created being as some misguided souls have been led to believe. Some will point to John 3:16 and say well Jesus is the only *begotten* Son of God and therefore He was created by God. This is a misunderstanding of the Greek word "mongenes" from the original Greek manuscript. Scholars state that the word mongenes does not mean begotten in the sense we beget (bear) children. Rather, the Greek word actually means "having no peer or unique". Jesus is not God the Father, but He is God the Son—unique in every sense.

God has revealed Himself through his Son Jesus. He has also revealed Himself by placing the Holy Spirit of God to dwell within us when we accept Jesus as Lord and Savior. God the

Father is the supreme authority and creator of all matter—seen and unseen.

Remember H_2O is the same regardless of where you find it. However, it can take on the form of a solid (ice), liquid (water), and gas (steam/vapor). Each is used for different purposes, but they are all commonly known as "water". I'm pleased that "water" can be used for different purposes—and I am also pleased that God chose to present Himself to us in different ways for our benefit.

CHAPTER 25

Bury Your Hypocrisy

I write this chapter as a "heads-up" to the immature Christian to not become discouraged when they hear others "sharing" their list of necessary "do's and don'ts" in order to be an acceptable Christian to God. Know this; your list is unique to you. What you need to work on in order to continue to improve, are not the same things that I, or anyone else, may need to refine, polish, or change. So while you may be inclined to reach out to another believer and ask for ideas about what you should do to make yourself a more complete and higher quality Christian, I urge you to self-analyze. No one knows you better than you do!

The other reason for including this chapter is to remind "seasoned" Christians to be judicious with their tongues in sharing personal opinions with those who are new or less sophisticated in their faith. This is something that even those occupying the pulpit, or in leadership positions, need to be consciously aware of when interacting with newer or less experienced disciples. Make sure you always attempt to lead by example by using Christ as the reference point, and that you do not come across as sanctimonious to these impressionable believers. Be helpful and explain that many "gray areas" exist within the faith and that asking God during prayer for direction is always the best approach. Thus, the message is to avoid being a hypocrite.

QUIT CONCERNING YOURSELF WITH OTHERS FAULTS.

The words of Jesus stress the importance of not being a hypocrite. Many times He states one of the worst things one can do is to constantly point at the "shortcomings" of others while ignoring your own "shortcomings". Consider the following from Matthew 7:3-5, "Why do you look at the speck of sawdust in your brother's eye and pay no attention to the plank in your own eye? How can you say to your brother, 'Let me take the speck out of your eye,' when all the time there is a plank in your own eye? You hypocrite, first take the plank out of your own eye, and then you will see clearly to remove the speck from your brother's eye."

It is my observation that this may be a primary area that most Christians still should be examining for improvement. It is often said that Christians are far too judgmental toward not only non-believers, but also fellow believers. Many say, and are correct, that Christians need to concern themselves more with their own actions instead of pointing out the actions of others. The time for self-examination is now.

God makes it abundantly clear that He despises hypocrites. These are people who attempt in deceiving others about their piety, when in all actuality they are nothing more than shallow followers of Christ. Sure they show up regularly for worship services, and they give generously in the "open". However, when they are certain others aren't looking, they are quick to put away their theatrical performance. You see, the Christian hypocrite is no different than other hypocrite; they don't practice what they preach either. Instead, the hypocrite is one who is constantly seeking the approval of others rather than God. Frequently, these hypocrites are quick to put down or poke fun at a fellow believer in front of others. This is done to increase their own self-esteem and to gain favor with the audience. Do not let hypocrites keep you from knowing God.

As previously noted, these (hypocrites) can even be "leaders" in the faith who are still more concerned with public persona rather than their actual character. These type of leaders are more focused on telling others what not to do (discouraging) to avoid hell, rather than focusing and encouraging others on what to do to achieve everlasting salvation. Yet, unfortunately, many church leaders are not aware that their messages are just like the Pharisees'. They are all too quick to tell you about requirements for church membership, doctrine, laws, rules—the very things that Jesus warned against. However, these leaders can't recognize that they are no different than the Pharisees that Jesus reprimanded continually for their preoccupation with legalism over spiritualism. They still can't acknowledge that all Christians are of one church body—Jesus Christ. These leaders attempt to point out that their worship center and/or faith structure is better than the "other guys" because they do this or that. Nevertheless, they fail to admit that the formation of various denominations of religious houses of worship is most definitely not from God, it is a man-made creation. Certainly go and worship where you like, but do not be deceived into believing that one denomination within Christianity has an advantage over another in the eyes of God.

Furthermore, do not look to others, or join the "gang", for acceptance or in order to ingratiate yourself in their approval. Rather, look to Christ alone for the acceptance and approval that you seek. Be yourself, not an actor on a stage. Look at what is said in these scriptures about hypocrisy: Luke 18:11, Matthew 6:2, Matthew 23:6-7, Matthew 23:5. Also examine the following from James 1:26 intently, "Those who consider themselves religious and yet do not keep a tight rein on their tongues deceive themselves, and their religion is worthless."

We only need to be like Jesus and avoid being like the Pharisees. Our thoughts should always be on Christ and doing as He suggests, not on following hypocrites who have agendas that do not line up with God's agenda. Be wise and always follow Christ's teachings over those of men.

CHAPTER 26

Final Thoughts

When some people read the Bible, they simply state it is nothing more than a book of antiquated rules. While others see the Bible as a book full of infinite wisdom or a book of "ways" to live their lives. Still, others read and see stories about ancient age extraordinary heroes who demonstrate the entire human experience. While others just see a mythological book similar to Homer's Odyssey. What do you say the Bible is? I would state that the Bible is a book about God, His desire to have a personal relationship with every human being, and His sacrifice of His Son upon the cross for the purpose of repairing and restoring our "DNA" to its original design in the future, so that we may have eternal salvation.

It is noted in Revelation just how Jesus will return to conquer and bind up Satan and reset the world. I'm being very simplistic here so feel free to read it on your own. However, what you will find is that it is Jesus who serves as the Redeemer who will find, save and heal those whom He loves—and that this entire process will take place over a thousand year period. At the end of the thousand year reign of Christ—who is to be worshipped (reserved only for God) as indicated in Revelation, God will then allow Satan to be set free and let him once again be allowed to deceive mankind for a little while. This is the final purification step—and if one passes all of this we then will be handed over to God the Father as His to either dwell in Heaven or inhabit the new earth that is described in Revelation.

JESUS SACRIFICE PUT US ON THE PATH TO RESTORING OUR PLANNED DNA.

The Bible does indeed contain rules and principles designed for us to live by in order to have the very best life possible. Ultimately though, the book is about relationships; relationships between man and his Creator, and people with people. It is a book designed to give us hope by showing us the love of God and the way back to God. The Old Testament points to the coming of a Messiah—Christ Jesus. The New Testament demonstrates that Jesus is Christ and wants to save us from ourselves—and the sins we harbor.

169

I have attempted my best to help anyone who took the time to read this book to gain a better understanding of God. Again, I did this out of a sincere belief that God had requested me to write these things down. As I said before, you are free to think whatever you wish about me and my motives, but I know I did as I felt I was instructed.

My purpose has been to share my "gift" of explaining, in simple language, what some key areas of Scripture mean and how it applies to your life. Only time will tell if my efforts prove fruitful and whether I have explained God's Word sufficiently.

I hope with all my being that one person, maybe a young person like one of my daughters, maybe a sibling, maybe an aunt or uncle or cousin, maybe a good friend or co-worker, or maybe even you a complete stranger has felt compelled to now turn their life over to Christ by making Him their Master, Lord, and Savior.

I do not know if I will ever be compelled by the Holy Spirit to ever write anything again along these lines. That is up to God. If this has helped you in any way I'd love to hear from you. My prayer is that you find the peace and happiness you have been seeking through the realization that only a genuine relationship with the Almighty can provide that to you. I stated at the beginning that I was in the pursuit of one soul. Only time will tell if I succeeded.

It is my hope through the wonderful work of God and the Second Coming of Jesus that our DNA will be restored to what God intended, and that sin will no longer dominate us.

I leave you with this from Proverbs 3:5-8 which reads, "**Trust in the Lord with all your heart, and lean not on your own understanding; In all your ways acknowledge Him, And He shall direct your paths, Do not be wise in your own eyes; Fear** (*ultimate respect*) **the Lord and depart from evil. It will be health to your flesh, and strength to your bones.**"

Finally, the wisest thing I can suggest is that you obtain the only life insurance policy that really matters. You don't have to spend a single dollar to purchase it as it is totally free of charge. However, you can only find this life insurance policy at one place—the **Everlasting Life Insurance Company!** By the way, it is only underwritten by one issuer—Almighty God.

All praise and glory to our Heavenly Father through our wonderful Christ Jesus. Amen!

Michael V. Gordon

Michael Gordon has been a health care administrator, business adviser, respiratory therapist, director of marketing, provider relations representative, urban farm consultant, athletic coach, recreation leader and wife and child support investigator—just to name a few. Born and raised in the Midwest, Michael has had an interest in writing all of his life. He wrote a book on Patient Satisfaction Surveys for the American Academy of Family Physicians, has written articles and been interviewed by health care journals on health business matters, been a speaker on health care reform, and was a photojournalist in college for the campus newspaper. Michael was named a

Kodak Photographic Award Winner in high school. He holds a degree in health care administration and in respiratory therapy. For several decades he has been reading, and researching about God and His word. Now he believes is the time to share his thoughts, in easy to understand language, on what he has discovered to inspire seekers and believers alike. Please feel free to visit Michael's web page, www.michaelvgordon.com for more information.